Computer System & Programming in C

First Edition

Yashavant Kanetkar

BPB PUBLICATIONS

FIRST EDITION 2017

Copyright © BPB Publications, INDIA

ISBN :978-93-8655-143-6

LIMITS OF LIABILITY AND DISCLAIMER OF WARRANTY

The Author and Publisher of this book have tried their best to ensure that the programmes, procedures and functions described in the book are correct. However, the author and the publishers make no warranty of any kind, expressed or implied, with regard to these programmes or the documentation contained in the book. The author and publisher shall not be liable in any event of any damages, incidental or consequential, in connection with, or arising out of the furnishing, performance or use of these programmes, procedures and functions. Product name mentioned are used for identification purposes only and may be trademarks of their respective companies.

All trademarks referred to in the book are acknowledged as properties of their respective owners.

Distributors:

BPB PUBLICATIONS
20, Ansari Road, Darya Ganj
New Delhi-110002
Ph: 23254990/23254991

BPB BOOK CENTRE
376 Old Lajpat Rai Market,
Delhi-110006
Ph: 23861747

COMPUTER BOOK CENTRE
12, Shrungar Shopping Centre,
M.G.Road, BENGALURU–560001
Ph: 25587923/25584641

DECCAN AGENCIES
4-3-329, Bank Street,
Hyderabad-500195
Ph: 24756967/24756400

MICRO MEDIA
Shop No. 5, Mahendra Chambers, 150
DN Rd. Next to Capital Cinema, V.T.
(C.S.T.) Station, MUMBAI-400 001 Ph:
22078296/22078297

Published by Manish Jain for BPB Publications, 20, Ansari Road, Darya Ganj, New Delhi-110002 and Printed him at Balaji Printer, New Delhi

Dedicated to baba
Who couldn't be here to see this day...

About the Author

Through his books and Quest Video Courseware DVDs on C, C++, Data Structures, VC++, .NET, Embedded Systems, etc. Yashavant Kanetkar has created, moulded and groomed lacs of IT careers in the last two decades. Yashavant's books and Quest DVDs have made a significant contribution in creating top-notch IT manpower in India and abroad.

Yashavant's books are globally recognized and millions of students / professionals have benefitted from them. Yashavant's books have been translated into Hindi, Gujarati, Japanese, Korean and Chinese languages. Many of his books are published in India, USA, Japan, Singapore, Korea and China.

Yashavant is a much sought after speaker in the IT field and has conducted seminars/workshops at TedEx, IITs, RECs and global software companies.

Yashavant has recently been honored with the prestigious "Distinguished Alumnus Award" by IIT Kanpur for his entrepreneurial, professional and academic excellence. This award was given to top 50 alumni of IIT Kanpur who have made significant contribution towards their profession and betterment of society in the last 50 years.

In recognition of his immense contribution to IT education in India, he has been awarded the "Best .NET Technical Contributor" and "Most Valuable Professional" awards by Microsoft for 5 successive years.

Yashavant holds a BE from VJTI Mumbai and M.Tech. from IIT Kanpur.

Contents

Best Sellers From The Desk Of Yashavant Kanetkar

#1 Best Seller

- ANSI C PROGRAMMING
- ASP.NET WEB SERVICES
- BPB LET US C (HINDI)
- COMPUTER PROGRAMMING & UTILIZATION
- C COLUMN COLLECTION
- C PEARLS
- C PROJECTS (W/CD)
- C#.NET FUNDAS (W/CD)
- C++.NET FUNDAS (W/CD)
- C/C++ & DATA STRUCTURES
- DATA STRUCTURES THROUGH C (W/CD)
- DATA STRUCTURES THROUGH C SOLUTION
- DATA STRUCTRES THOUGH C++ (W/CD)
- DIRECTX GAME PROGRAMMING FUNDAS (W/CD)
- EXPLORING C
- GO EMBEDDED (W/CD)
- GRAPHICS UNDER C
- INTRODUCTION TO OOPS & C ++
- INTERVIEW QUESTIONS IN C & C ++PROG
- LET US JAVA
- LET US C
- LET US C SOLUTIONS
- LET US C WORK BOOK
- LET US C ++
- LET US C ++ SOLUTIONS
- LET US C#
- PROGRAMMING EXPERTISE IN BASIC
- TEST YOUR C SKILLS
- TEST YOUR C ++ SKILLS
- TEST YOUR C#.NET SKILLS
- TEST YOUR UNIX SKILLS
- TEST YOUR VB.NET SKILLS PART-1
- TEST YOUR VB. NET SKILLS PART -2
- UNDERSTANDING POINTERS IN C
- UNDOCUMETED DOS THROUGH C
- UNDOCUMENTED DOS THROUGH C
- UNIX SHELL PROGRAMMING
- VC++ GEMS (W/CD)
- VC ++, COM & BEYOND (W/CD)
- VISUAL C++ PROJECTS (W/CD)
- WORKING WITH C
- WRITTEN TSR'S THROUGH C
- WRITTEN WINDOWS DEVICE DRIVERS (W/CD)
- WRITTEN TEST QUES.IN C PROGRAMMING
- WRITTEN TEST QUES.IN DATA STRUCTURES
- WRITTEN TEST QUES.IN JAVA PROGRAMMING

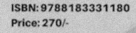   

Unit 1

Fundamentals of Computers

- Introduction to Digital Computer
  Input Unit
  Central Processing Unit (CPU)
  Output Unit
- Classification of Computers
- Operating System
- Functions of an Operating System
- Types of Operating Systems
- Numbering Systems
- Conversion
- Binary Arithmetic
- Programming Basics
- Basic Model of Computation
- Algorithms
- Flowchart
- Programming Languages
- Stages in the Development of a C Program
  Developing the Program
  Compiling the Program
  Linking the Program
  Testing the Program
  Documenting the Program
- Sample Algorithms and Flowcharts
  Exchanging Values of Two Variables
  Summation of a set of Numbers
  Reversing Digits of an Integer
- Exercise

Before we begin writing programs in C, it would be necessary to understand what is a Digital Computer, how it operates, what are its functional components and what different types of Digital Computers exist.

It would also be interesting to know about the most basic program which makes digital computer work, i.e. the Operating System. Since Digital Computers internally use a Binary Numbering System, it is necessary to know the details of this numbering system before we begin programming.

Ultimately a program is nothing but a systematic representation of the algorithm that solves a particular problem. So in this chapter we would also be looking at different approaches to problem solving.

Introduction to Digital Computer

A Digital Computer is an electronic device that performs calculations and logical operations on quantities represented as digits. The quantities are represented in binary numbering system and the calculations and logical operations are performed as per the instructions given in a program. The program is also represented using binary notation.

(a) A digital computer carries out the following five operations:

(a) Receives input data.

(b) Stores data/instructions in its memory and uses them as required.

(c) Processes data to obtain useful information.

(d) Generates output.

(e) Controls above four steps.

To carry out the above functions every digital computer consists of certain functional components. These are shown in Figure 1.1. Let us now understand the purpose of each functional component.

Input Unit

This unit contains devices with the help of which we enter data and programs into the computer. Thus this unit acts as a link between the user and the computer. The most common device is keyboard. But computer can also read data from files on the disk or receive it from other computers connected to a network.

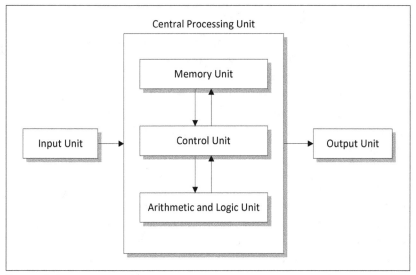

Figure 1.1

Central Processing Unit (CPU)

CPU is the most important part of the computer. It acts like a brain of the computer. It performs different types of operations on the input data as per the instructions given in the program. It stores the intermediate results created during these operations and sends the final results to the output devices. A CPU consists of following three components:

(a) Arithmetic Logic Unit (ALU): This unit is responsible for carrying out Arithmetic and Logical operations. Logical operations consist of comparison between entities.

(b) Memory Unit: This unit can store input data, program instructions, intermediate and final results.

(c) Control Unit: This unit itself doesn't carry out any data processing operations. But, as its name suggests, it manages and coordinates the operations of all other parts of the digital computer.

Output Unit

This unit contains devices with the help of which we get the information from the computer. This unit is a link between the computer and the users. Output devices translate the computer's output into a form understandable by the users.

Classification of Computers

There are different types of computers based on requirements of users and organizations. Though they vary largely in processing power, resources, capabilities, size and cost all of them follow the same basic logical structure that we discussed in the previous section and perform the same five basic operations for converting raw input data into useful information. Different types of computers available today are discussed below in brief.

Laptop Computer

A laptop is a small, portable personal computer. It can be folded like a notebook with the lower part consisting of an alphanumeric keyboard and the upper part consisting of a thin LCD or LED screen. The notebook should be opened to use it. Since laptops can be folded shut they are easy to transport. Laptops are commonly used at work, in education, in playing games, Internet surfing, for personal multimedia and general home computer use.

Today a standard laptop combines the components, inputs, outputs, and capabilities of a desktop computer. These include a processor, memory, display screen (or touch screen), keyboard, hard disk drive, touchpad (mouse), speakers, webcam and microphone. Laptops can be powered either from an internal battery or by an external power supply from an AC adapter. Processor speed and memory capacity of a laptop varies across manufacturers, models and price points.

Personal Computer (PC)

A PC is a small, relatively inexpensive computer designed for an individual user. A PC uses a microprocessor that has the entire CPU on one chip. PCs are used by businesses typically for word processing, accounting, preparing presentation and spreadsheets and for running simple database management applications. In offices PCs are connected to the office network.

At home, PCs are used for playing games, surfing the Internet and doing online purchases.

Today the processing, memory sizes and multimedia capabilities of high-end PC models of popular brands like Lenevo, Dell, Apple, etc. matches with low-end workstations by Hewlett-Packard, and Dell.

Workstation

Workstation is a computer used for graphics based engineering applications (CAD/CAM), high-end desktop publishing, serious software development, etc. Workstations have good computing power and high quality graphics capabilities. To support these workstations generally come with a large, high-resolution graphics screen, large amount of RAM, inbuilt network support, and high hard disk capacity. Workstations can work as stand-alone machines, but are usually connected to a network. Common operating systems for workstations are Linux and Windows NT.

Minicomputer

It is a midsize computer system capable of supporting up to 250 users simultaneously. It has the ability of running multiple programs of multiple users simultaneously. These are usually resource rich systems since it has to support multiple users simultaneously.

Mainframe Computer

Mainframe computers are very large in size and can support literally thousands of users simultaneously. Mainframe executes many programs concurrently. Mainframe computers are typically used for building weather prediction models, detect Tsunamis and earthquakes, building drug development research models, etc.

Supercomputer

Supercomputers are extremely fast computers and can process tons of data very quickly. These are used in applications where huge amount of mathematical calculations are required. These include big data analysis, scientific and engineering simulations, animation movies, analysis of geological data, land use planning etc.

Operating System

An operating system (OS) is software that acts as an interface between user and the computer hardware (refer Figure 1.2). It also manages computer hardware and software resources and provides common services for computer programs. All computer programs require an operating system to function. An OS also controls and monitors the execution of all other programs that reside in the computer system including application programs and other system software.

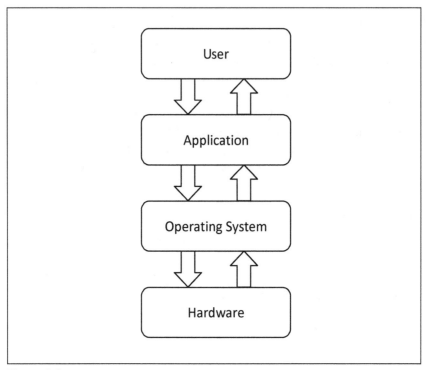

Figure 1.2

Functions of an Operating System

A typical OS performs the following function:

(a) It makes it convenient for the user to use the computer system in an easy and efficient manner. For example, the icons in Windows makes it intuitive for the user to carry out operations like starting a program, terminating a program, taking printouts, saving files, opening new files, etc.

(b) It hides the details of the hardware resources from the users. User doesn't have to figure out the details like how to allocate space for a file on the disk, how to create directories, etc.

(c) It manages resources like disk space and memory of a computer system. The OS ensures that all running programs get a fair space in memory and disk.

(d) It does process management for different running programs. It keeps track of which process is using which resource, grants resource requests, resolves conflicting requests like two programs trying to print on the same printer.

(e) It provides device driver programs to drive different standard Input / Output devices like monitor, keyboard, mouse, etc.

(f) It provides networking components to let the computer and the applications in it to participate in networking to access and share hardware and software resources. For example, it lets you access Internet through a modem connected to the server in the network.

(g) It provides security by preventing unauthorized access to programs and data by means of passwords, firewalls and file permissions.

Types of Operating Systems

Based on the user requirements and the hardware different Operating Systems have come into existence. These are as follows:

(a) MS-DOS: It was a very popular system developed for a stand-alone PC. It lost its significance when GUI and networking became mainstream and was slowly phased out. MS-DOS was a single-user, single tasking OS, i.e. it allowed only one user to execute one program at a time. To launch another program it was necessary to terminate the currently running program.

(b) Windows OS: Microsoft Windows is an operating system designed by Microsoft Corporation for Intel architecture based computers. Over the years several versions of it have come into existence including Windows 3.1, Windows 95, Windows 98, Windows 2000, Windows XP, Windows Vista, Windows 7, Windows 8 and Windows 10. Windows is a single user multitasking OS, i.e. one user can run several programs in it concurrently. For example, one can run Excel, PowerPoint, Word and Calculator simultaneously.

(c) Windows NT: This is the server version of Windows. As its name suggests it can serve several users simultaneously in a networked environment.

(d) Linux: Linux originated in 1991, as a project of Linus Torvalds, while a university student in Finland. It has grown to its current state through contributions from volunteers worldwide. Linux is Unix-like. Since it is an open-source OS, its source code is available free of cost. This has resulted in its use on a wide range of computing machinery from supercomputers to smart-watches. Although Linux is not very popularly used on desktops or laptops, it has been widely adopted for use in servers and embedded systems such as cell phones. All

Android phones, for example use Linux OS. Like Windows NT, Linux also supports multiple users and multiple programs simultaneously.

Numbering Systems

When we talk about numbering systems we are really talking about the base of the numbering system. Base represents the number of digits that one can use before one runs out of digits. For example, in decimal numbering system we have 10 digits from 0 to 9. When we run out of digits we put a 1 in the columns to the left—the ten's column—and start again in the one's column with 0.

Like decimal numbering system there are others like octal, hexadecimal and binary. Octal numbering system uses 8 digits from 0 to 7, hexadecimal uses 16 digits from 0 to 9 and A to F and binary uses 2 digits from 0 to 1. In hexadecimal numbering system A to F are used to represent numbers from 10 to 15. Figure 1.3 shows how numbers are constructed in these different numbering systems.

Decimal	Octal	Hexadecimal	Binary
0	0	0	0
1	1	1	1
2	2	2	10
.	.	.	11
.	.	.	100
9	7	9	101
10	10	A	110
11	11	B	111
12	..	.	1000
..	..	.	....
19	77	F	
20	100	10	
21	101	11	
..	...	12	
	...	..	
	107	19	
	110	1A	
	...	1B	
		..	

Figure 1.3

Conversion

It is often necessary to convert a number from one numbering system to another. To convert a number in a given numbering system to decimal numbering system, we have to multiply each digit of the number with a suitable power of the base of that numbering system. For example to convert from binary to decimal we have to multiply by powers of 2, to convert from octal to decimal we have to multiply with powers of 8 and to convert from hexadecimal to decimal we have to multiply by powers of 16. This is illustrated in the examples below.

Conversion of binary 1011 to decimal:

$$1 \times 2^3 + 0 \times 2^2 + 1 \times 2^1 + 1 \times 2^0 = 8 + 0 + 2 + 0 = 10$$

Thus binary 1011 is equal to decimal 10.

Conversion of octal 127 to decimal:

$$1 \times 8^2 + 2 \times 8^1 + 7 \times 8^0 = 36 + 16 + 7 = 59$$

Thus octal 127 is equal to decimal 59.

Conversion of hexadecimal A21 to decimal:

$$A \times 16^2 + 2 \times 16^1 + 1 \times 16^0 = 2560 + 32 + 1 = 2539$$

Thus hexadecimal A21 is equal to decimal 2539.

If we are to convert a number from decimal numbering system to other numbering systems then we have to go on di

Since computers understand binary and C language understands decimal, octal and hexadecimal, we are often required to convert from binary to these numbering systems. This involves successive divisions by base of the target numbering system till we do not get a 0, obtaining remainders, and finally writing remainders in the reverse order. Figure 1.4 shows this procedure.

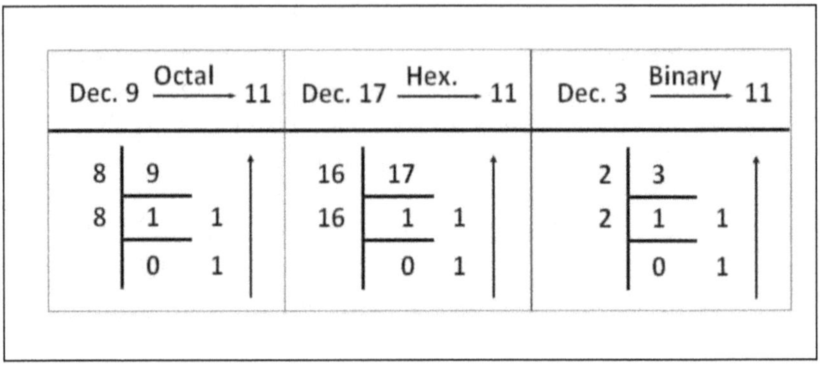

Dec. 9 $\dfrac{\text{Octal}}{}$ 11		Dec. 17 $\dfrac{\text{Hex.}}{}$ 11		Dec. 3 $\dfrac{\text{Binary}}{}$ 11	
8	9	16	17	2	3
8	1 1	16	1 1	2	1 1
	0 1		0 1		0 1

Figure 1.4

Binary Arithmetic

Binary arithmetic involves four operations—Addition, Subtraction, Multiplication and Division. Let us see one by one how these operations are performed.

Binary Addition

There are four rules of binary addition. These are shown in Figure 1.5.

Rule	x + y	Sum	Carry
1	0 + 0	0	0
2	0 + 1	1	0
3	1 + 0	1	0
4	1 + 1	0	1

Figure 1.5

In the last rule the binary addition of 1 + 1 gives 10, i.e. 0 is written in the given column and 1 is carried over to the next column.

Given below is an example of binary addition of two numbers.

10101010 + 01010111 =

```
     1111      Carry
  10101010     (decimal 170)
+ 01000111     (decimal 71)
  _____
  11110001     (decimal 241)
```

Binary Subtraction

The way binary addition involves a carry, binary subtraction involves a borrow. The rules for binary subtraction are shown in Figure 1.6.

Rule	x - y	Difference	Borrow
1	0 - 0	0	0
2	0 - 1	0	1
3	1 - 0	1	0
4	1 - 1	0	0

Figure 1.6

In the second rule the binary subtraction of 0 - 1 gives 0 and borrows 1 from the previous column.

Given below is an example of binary subtraction of two numbers.

10101010 - 01010111 = 01100011

```
     010      Borrow
 10101010     (decimal 170)
- 01000111    (decimal 71)
_____
 01100011     (decimal 99)
```

Binary Multiplication

Binary multiplication is similar to decimal multiplication. It is simpler than decimal multiplication because only 0s and 1s are involved. The rules of binary multiplication are shown in Figure 1.7.

Rule	a x b	Result
1	0 x 0	0
2	0 x 1	0
3	1 x 0	0
4	1 x 1	1

Figure 1.7

Given below is an example of binary multiplication of two numbers.

10101010 x 01010111 = 10111100100110

```
        10101010    (decimal 170)
      x 01000111    (decimal 71)
    _____
        10101010
        10101010
        10101010
        00000000
        00000000
        00000000
    +   10101010
    _____
    10111100100110   (decimal 12070)
```

Binary Division

Binary division is similar to decimal division. It is carried out using the long division procedure. Given below is an example of binary division of two numbers.

10101010 / 01010111 gives quotient of 10 (decimal 2) and remainder 1110 (decimal 28).

```
                        1 0
            1000111 / 10101010
                    /  1000111
                      _____
                       00011100
                       00000000
                      _____
                       00011100
```

Programming Basics

Attempting to learn a programming language before having any idea about the basic model of computation, the way to evolve a solution, the way to represent it and the overall program development process would be like putting a horse before the cart. Hence we would now focus on these topics and create a solid background before we venture into C programming. Let us begin with the computation model.

Basic Model of Computation

Really speaking, the idea of computing is not new to any of us. Each one of us have used mainly used pencil and paper to do fundamental computing operations like addition, subtraction, multiplication, division or slightly more complex operations like computing lengths, areas, volumes etc. While performing all these computations we follow some definite, unambiguous set of rules. Similarly when we do computation using a computer we follow a certain set of rules. The basic model of computation involves input, process and output. These are shown in Figure 1.8.

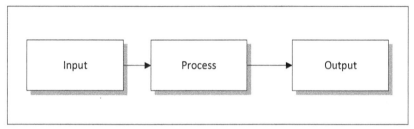

Figure 1.8

The input is received using input devices like keyboard, mouse, touch screen, etc. Once the input is received it is processed using the Central Processing Unit (CPU) of the computer and the result is then displayed using the output devices like VDU, printer, plotter, etc. The processing involves performing arithmetic operation and logical comparison operations (like a < b, c >= d, etc.). In addition to this the CPU also controls operations of input / output devices and memory. While solving any problem using a computer we need to explicitly write down the steps keeping the above model of computation in mind. These explicit steps for solving a given computing problem, is called an Algorithm. Let us now study the purpose of an algorithm in general.

Algorithms

As mentioned in the previous section, the explicit set of steps for solving a given computing problem is called an algorithm. Thus algorithms are used as a means of communication for specifying solutions to computational problems, unambiguously, so that others can understand the solutions. More precisely, an algorithm is a sequence of instructions that act on some input data to produce some output in a finite number of steps. An algorithm must have the following properties:

(a) Input – An algorithm must receive some input data supplied externally.

(b) Output – An algorithm must produce at least one output as the result.

(c) Finiteness – No matter what is the input, the algorithm must terminate after a finite number of steps. For example, a procedure which goes on performing a series of steps infinitely is not an algorithm.

(d) Definiteness – The steps to be performed in the algorithm must be clear and unambiguous.

(e) Effectiveness – One must be able to perform the steps in the algorithm without applying any intelligence. For example, the step— Select three numbers which form a Pythogorian triplet—is not effective.

While creating an algorithm it is important to choose an appropriate model of computation to describe an algorithm. Based on the choice we make, the type of computations that can be carried out in the model gets decided. For example, if our computational model contains only ruler and compass, then using these primitives we can write down explicit algorithms for drawing a line segment of specific length, bisecting it, drawing an angle, bisecting it, etc. However, using these primitives we would not be able to trisect an angle. For doing this we would need additional primitives like a protractor. For arithmetic computations we can use various computing models like calculators. As you can imagine, with each of these models of computing, the rules for specifying a solution (algorithms) are different. Therefore, it is important to first choose an appropriate model of computation while creating algorithms.

There are two ways in which we can describe an algorithm that is used for solving a problem:

(a) Describe it in the form of step by step procedure written in textual form

(b) Describe it in the form of a figure called Flowchart

We are quite habituated to describing a step by step procedure in textual form. However, when it comes to describing the procedure using a flowchart we need to understand the common rules followed for drawing it. Let us now try to understand them.

Flowchart

A flowchart describes an algorithm by showing the different steps in it as boxes of various shapes connected using arrows to indicate their order. Thus a flowchart gives a diagrammatic representation of a step-by-step solution to a given problem. Flowcharts are extensively used to describe an algorithm, as "a picture is worth a thousand words". A typical flowchart uses the symbols shown in Figure 1.9 to represent different tasks that are contained in an algorithm.

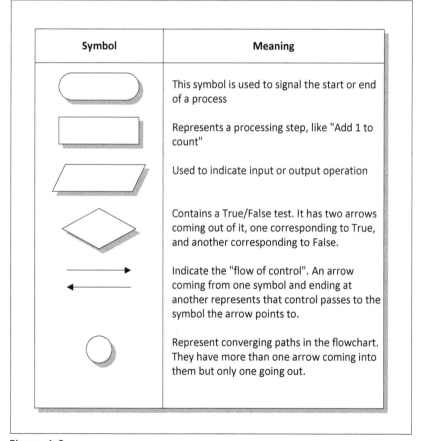

Symbol	Meaning
	This symbol is used to signal the start or end of a process
	Represents a processing step, like "Add 1 to count"
	Used to indicate input or output operation
	Contains a True/False test. It has two arrows coming out of it, one corresponding to True, and another corresponding to False.
	Indicate the "flow of control". An arrow coming from one symbol and ending at another represents that control passes to the symbol the arrow points to.
	Represent converging paths in the flowchart. They have more than one arrow coming into them but only one going out.

Figure 1.9

Let us now take some example and try to describe an algorithm for it in both forms—textual and flowchart. Suppose we wish to find out the biggest of three numbers. Given below is an algorithm and flowchart for it, both of which are self-explanatory. It would be a good idea to take any three numbers and try the algorithm and the flowchart on them.

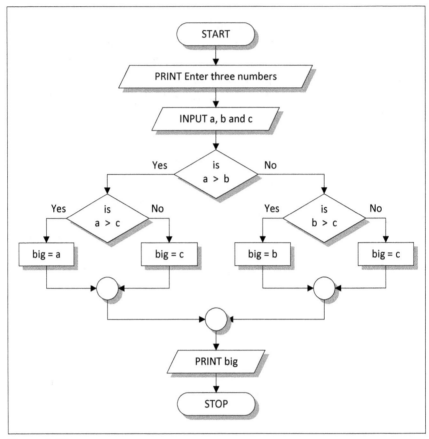

Figure 1.10

Algorithm:

Step 1: Enter three numbers, say a, b, c

Step 2: Check if a > b

        If so, check if b > c

                If so, set big = b

                If not, set big = c

        If not, check if a > c

                If so, set big = a

                If not, set big = c

Step 3: Print big

Step 4: Exit

Once an algorithm is ready in textual or flowchart form we can easily convert it into a computer program using the grammar rules (syntax) of a programming language. Before we see how this is done, it would be appropriate to know some details about programming languages.

Programming Languages

A Computer understands only 0s and 1s. Hence it has to be instructed through a program only in terms of 0s and 1s. Such a program is called a Machine Language program. As you can appreciate, writing programs in machine language is difficult, tedious and error-prone.

To overcome this difficulty, a language called Assembly Language was invented. In a program written in this language mnemonic symbols (abbreviations) are used instead of 0s and 1s. For example, ADD is used for addition, SUB for subtraction, CMP for comparison, etc. Naturally it is easy to remember these mnemonics as compared to their equivalent 0s and 1s. However, the computer doesn't understand these mnemonics. Therefore, it is necessary to convert an assembly language program into machine language before it is executed. This translation task is done through a converter program called Assembler.

A language in which each statement or an instruction is directly translated into a single machine instruction is known as a Low-level language. Each mnemonic of an assembly language has a unique machine code. Hence Assembly language is a low-level language. Machine language is also a low-level language. The instructions that one Microprocessor (CPU) can understand are different than those understood by another. This is because internal architecture of each microprocessor is different. Hence the machine language and correspondingly the assembly language for each microprocessor are different. Thus, machine language and assembly language for Intel Pentium microprocessor are different than those for Atmel ATmega32 microprocessor. This means assembly language program written for one microprocessor cannot be used on another microprocessor. In other words it is not portable. Hence, to write an assembly language program, a programmer must have detailed knowledge of the instruction set of the particular microprocessor, its internal architecture, registers, and connection of peripherals to ports etc.

To overcome these difficulties associated with assembly language, High-level languages have been developed. In a high level language instead of mnemonics English-like instructions are used. Instructions in these languages permit programmers to describe tasks in the forms that are problem-oriented rather than machine-oriented. Moreover, one does not have to possess knowledge of the architecture of the microprocessor to be able write programs in these languages. Some of the popular high-level languages include BASIC, FORTRAN, Pascal, COBOL, C, C++, Java, C#, etc. The differences that exist between these languages are beyond the scope of this book. In this book we would be concentrating only on learning one of the most popular and widely used high-level language, namely C.

A program written in a high level language is converted into machine language program using software called Compiler. These compilers are targeted for different microprocessors. For example, the Visual Studio compiler can convert a C language program into machine language instructions that can be understood by Intel microprocessors. Similarly, the gcc complier can convert a C language program into machine language instructions that can be understood by ATmega32.

Stages in the Development of a C Program

One has to go through several stages before a program gets ready to be used on a computer. These stages are discussed below. The entire process is also shown in Figure 1.11 in the form of a flowchart to help understand the process better.

Developing the Program

The task of developing a program for a particular problem involves a careful study of the problem with an aim to clearly identify the output desired from the program and input that would be provided to it. For example, while developing a program to solve a quadratic equation, input would be the coefficients and output would be the roots of the quadratic equation. Once this is done the next task is to prepare an algorithm or a flowchart (or both) that details the steps to be carried out to obtain the desired output from the input provided. Finally we need to convert this algorithm / flowchart into a C language program. Once the program is ready, we need to type it into a computer and store in a file on the disk.

Compiling the Program

The next step is to translate the C language program into machine language. This is done using a C compiler. The converted code in machine language is often called object code. If there are any errors in your program, then the compiler prints the appropriate messages pointing out these errors and the compilation process terminates. We now need to identify the error prone portion of the program and make the necessary corrections and repeat the compilation process.

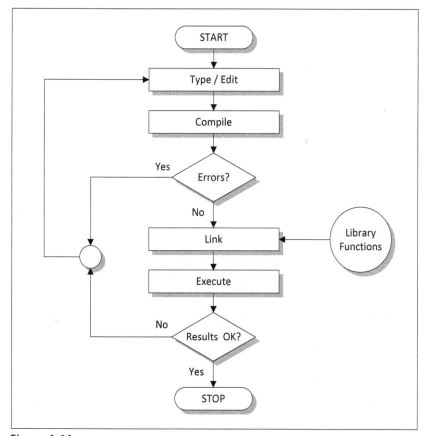

Figure 1.11

Linking the Program

Once the program is successfully compiled, the machine language version of our C program is ready. However, it is not in the form in which we can execute it. This is because in our program we may have used certain ready-made instructions (called Library Functions). These functions are usually provided by companies that create compilers. These companies develop these functions, compile them separately and make them available to us in machine language form. So now there is a need to combine our program's machine language code with library functions' machine language code. This is done using a program called **Linker**. The combined code is called executable code and is in a form which can be executed on a machine.

Testing the Program

The next stage in the development of a program is called Testing. In this stage the program is thoroughly tested for its correctness. For this the program is executed with all possible values of input data for which results are known. If the program's output matches with the known results then the program is declared as correct. If not, then the program is scanned thoroughly to locate the logical errors and is duly rectified. At times, the algorithm and flowchart are also reviewed to locate the errors.

Documenting the Program

The final stage in the development of a program is Documentation. In this stage all the relevant and important information about the program is recorded in such a manner that anyone who is later on required to upgrade or modify this program would be able to understand its intended purpose and the logic used to achieve this purpose.

Sample Algorithms and Flowcharts

In one of the previous sections we saw what are algorithms and flowcharts and how they can be used as aids for describing and depicting a solution to any programming problem. However, just understanding the purpose of algorithms and flowcharts is not enough. We must be able to actually use them to solve programming problems. Best way to do this is to go ahead and use them in solving some problems. With that view given below are some sample problems and their solutions in the form of algorithms and flowcharts

Exchanging Values of Two Variables

If values of two variables are input through the keyboard, draw a flowchart and write an algorithm for exchanging the contents of two variables.

Flowchart:

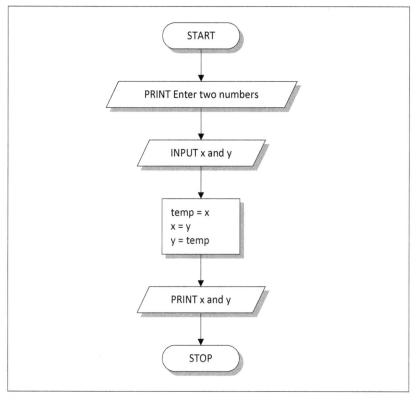

Figure 1.12

Algorithm:

Step 1: Declare x, y and temp as integer variables

Step 2: Enter values of two variables i.e. x and y

Step 3: Exchange values of two variables

Step 4: Print values of variables x and y

Summation of a Set of Numbers

If values of 'n' number of variables are input through the keyboard, draw a flowchart and write an algorithm for finding summation of a set of 'n' numbers.

Flowchart:

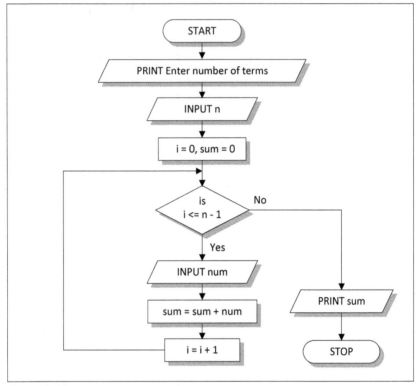

Figure 1.13

Algorithm:

Step 1: Enter number of terms (say n) whose sum is to be calculated

Step 2: Initialize i = 0 and sum = 0

Step 3: Repeat steps 4, 5, 6 while i <= n – 1

Step 4: Enter each number i.e. num

Step 5: Calculate sum using sum = sum + num

Step 6: Increment loop counter using i = i + 1

      [End of Step 3 Loop]

Step 7: Print sum

Step 8: Exit

Reversing Digits of an Integer

If a 5-digit number is input through the keyboard, draw a flowchart and write an algorithm to calculate reverse of that number.

Flowchart:

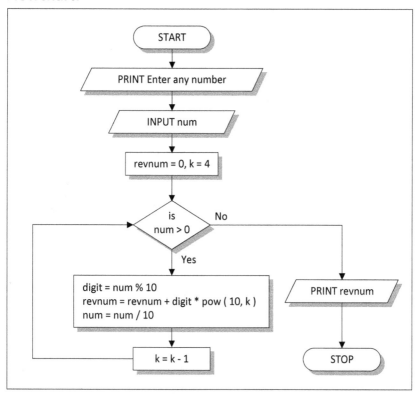

Figure 1.14

Algorithm:

Step 1: Enter a number (say num) whose reverse is to be calculated

Step 2: Initialize revnum = 0, k = 4

Step 3: Repeat Steps 4, 5, 6, 7 while num > 0

Step 4: Find last digit using digit = num % 10

Step 5: Update revnum using revnum = revnum + digit * 10 raised to k

Step 6: Reduce the number using num = num / 10

Step 7: Increment k using k = k - 1

[End of Step 3 Loop]

Step 7: Print revnum

Step 8: Exit

Exercise

[A] Attempt the following:

(a) If three numbers are input through the keyboard, draw a flowchart and write an algorithm for finding the minimum of these three numbers.

(b) If a number is input through the keyboard, draw a flowchart and write an algorithm for finding out whether the number is odd or even.

(c) Draw a flowchart and write an algorithm for calculating and printing out a table of 15.

(d) Draw a flowchart and write an algorithm for finding out squares and cubes of all numbers from 1 to 20.

(e) Carry out the following conversions:

Convert 1278 into its Hexadecimal equivalent.

Convert 322 into its Binary equivalent.

Convert 10101111 into its decimal equivalent.

Convert 4423 into its Octal equivalent.

[B] Pick up the correct alternative for each of the following.

(a) Which of the following is NOT true about an Operating System.
    (1) It acts as a manager
    (2) It acts as a command processor
    (3) It acts as a controller
    (4) It acts as a compiler

(b) Multi-user multi-tasking OS means
    (1) Multiple users can perform multiple tasks at a time
    (2) Multiple tasks can be performed by the user
    (3) Multiple users can perform the same task at a time
    (4) None of the above

(c) Windows NT is a
    (1) Single-user, single tasking OS
    (2) Multi-user, multitasking OS

(3) Single-user, multitasking OS

(4) Real-time OS

(d) Memory management, process control are the functions of

(1) OS kernel

(2) Microprocessor

(3) Scheduler

(4) None of the above

[C] State whether the following statements are True or False:

(a) A linker is used to combine two different C programs.

(b) A compiler converts an assembly language program into a machine language program.

(c) An assembly language program is converted into a machine language program using an assembler.

(d) An algorithm is developed on the basis of a C program.

(e) An algorithm and a flowchart are different ways of representing the same solution.

(f) Linking precedes the compilation operation.

(g) A C program uses mnemonics to represent instructions.

(h) Whether we write a program in assembly language or in a C language it has to be converted into machine language before it can get executed.

(i) An algorithm need not have the scalability property.

(j) An algorithm must terminate after a finite number of steps.

(k) An algorithm must receive some input data and must produce at least one output as the result.

(l) While creating an algorithm an appropriate model of computation must be chosen to describe it.

(m) In a flowchart, a processing step is represented using a Parallelogram.

(n) In a flowchart, the Input or Output operation is represented using a Rhombus.

(o) Instructions in a low-level language get translated into multiple machine instructions.

(p) Assembly language instructions for all microprocessors are same.

(q) Assembly language program written for one microprocessor can be used on another microprocessor.

[D] Match the following pairs of flowchart symbols and their purpose:

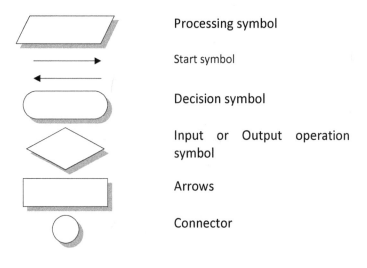

Processing symbol

Start symbol

Decision symbol

Input or Output operation symbol

Arrows

Connector

Unit 2

Fundamentals of C Programming

- Getting Started with C
  The C Character Set
  Constants, Variables and Keywords
  Types of C Constants
  Rules for Constructing Integer Constants
  Integers, *long* and *short*
  Integers, *signed* and *unsigned*
  Rules for Constructing Real Constants
  Rules for Constructing Character Constants
  Types of C Variables
  Rules for Constructing Variable Names
  C Keywords
- The First C Program
  Form of a C Program
  Comments in a C Program
  What is *main( )*?
  Variables and their Usage
  printf( ) and its Purpose
  Compilation and Execution
- Receiving Input
- Arithmetic Instruction
- Integer and Float Conversions
- Type Conversion in Assignments
- More Operators
- Hierarchy of Operations
- Associativity of Operators
- Storage Classes in C
  Automatic Storage Class
  Register Storage Class
  Static Storage Class
  External Storage Class
- Exercise

Before we can begin to write serious programs in C, it would be interesting to find out what really is C, how it came into existence and how does it compare with other programming languages. In this chapter, we would briefly outline these issues.

Four important aspects of any language are the way it stores data, the way it operates upon this data, how it accomplishes input and output, and how it lets you control the sequence of execution of instructions in a program. We would discuss the first three of these building blocks in this chapter.

Getting Started with C

C is a programming language developed at AT & T's Bell Laboratories of USA in 1972. It was designed by a man named Dennis Ritchie.

There is a close analogy between learning English language and learning C language. The classical method of learning English is to first learn the alphabets used in the language, then learn to combine these alphabets to form words, which, in turn, are combined to form sentences and sentences are combined to form paragraphs.

Learning C is similar and easier. Instead of straight-away learning how to write programs, we must first know what alphabets, numbers and special symbols are used in C, then how using them, constants, variables and keywords are constructed, and finally, how are these combined to form an instruction. A group of instructions would be combined later on to form a program. This is illustrated in the Figure 2.1.

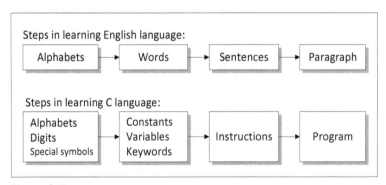

Figure 2.1

The C Character Set

A character denotes any alphabet, digit or special symbol used to represent information. Figure 2.2 shows the valid alphabets, numbers and special symbols allowed in C.

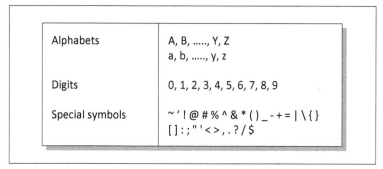

Alphabets	A, B, ..., Y, Z a, b, ..., y, z
Digits	0, 1, 2, 3, 4, 5, 6, 7, 8, 9
Special symbols	~ ' ! @ # % ^ & * ( ) _ - + = | \ { } [ ] : ; " ' < > , . ? / $

Figure 2.2

Constants, Variables and Keywords

The alphabets, digits and special symbols when properly combined form constants, variables and keywords. Let us now understand the meaning of each of them. A constant is an entity that doesn't change, whereas, a variable is an entity that may change. A keyword is a word that carries special meaning.

In any C program we typically do lots of calculations. The results of these calculations are stored in computer's memory. Like human memory, the computer's memory also consists of millions of cells. The calculated values are stored in these memory cells. To make the retrieval and usage of these values easy, these memory cells (also called memory locations) are given names. Since the value stored in each location may change, the names given to these locations are called variable names. Let us understand this with the help of an example.

Consider the memory locations shown in Figure 2.3. Here 3 is stored in a memory location and a name **x** is given to it. Then we have assigned a new value 5 to the same memory location **x**. This would overwrite the earlier value 3, since a memory location can hold only one value at a time.

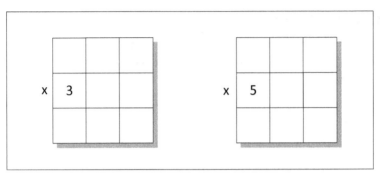

Figure 2.3

Since the location whose name is **x** can hold different values at different times **x** is known as a variable (or a variable name). As against this, 3 or 5 do not change, hence are known as constants.

In programming languages, constants are often called literals, whereas, variables are called identifiers.

Now that we understand the constants and the variables, let us see what different types of constants and variables exist in C.

Types of C Constants

C constants can be divided into two major categories:

(a) Primary Constants

(b) Secondary Constants

These constants are further categorized as shown in Figure 2.4.

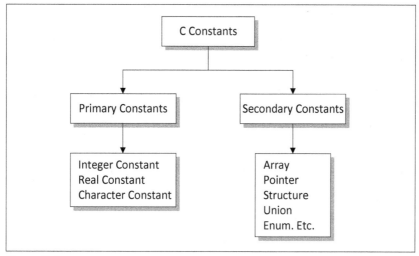

Figure 2.4

At this stage, we would restrict our discussion to only Primary constants, namely, Integer, Real and Character constants. Let us see the details of each of these constants. For constructing these different types of constants, certain rules have been laid down. These rules are as under:

Rules for Constructing Integer Constants

(a) An integer constant must have at least one digit.

(b) It must not have a decimal point.

(c) It can be either positive or negative.

(d) If no sign precedes an integer constant, it is assumed to be positive.

(e) No commas or blanks are allowed within an integer constant.

(f) The allowable range for integer constants is -2147483648 to +2147483647.

Truly speaking, the range of an Integer constant depends upon the compiler. For compilers like Visual Studio, gcc, it is -2147483648 to +214748364, whereas for compilers like Turbo C or Turbo C++ the range is -32768 to +32767.

Ex.: 426
    +782
    -8000
    -7605

Integers, *long* and *short*

C offers a variation of the integer data type that provides what are called **short** and **long** integer values. The intention of providing these variations is to provide integers with different ranges wherever possible. Though not a rule, **short** and **long** integers would usually occupy two and four bytes respectively. Each compiler can decide appropriate sizes depending on the operating system and hardware, for which it is being written, subject to the following rules:

(a) **short**s are at least 2 bytes big

(b) **long**s are at least 4 bytes big

(c) **short**s are never bigger than **int**s

(d) **int**s are never bigger than **long**s

The range for 2-byte integers is -32768 to +32768, whereas for 4-byte integers it is from -2147483648 to +2147483647

Integers, signed and *unsigned*

Sometimes, we know in advance that the value stored in a given integer variable will always be positive—when it is being used to only count things like say number of students. In such cases we can use **unsigned integers**. When we do so the range of permissible short integer values will shift from the range -32768 to +32767 to 0 to 65535. Similarly the range for 4-byte integers would shift from −2147483648 to +2147483647 to the range 0 to 4294967295.

Rules for Constructing Real Constants

Real constants are often called Floating Point constants or just floats. Following rules must be observed while constructing real constants expressed in fractional form:

(a) A real constant must have at least one digit.

(b) It must have a decimal point.

(c) It could be either positive or negative.

(d) Default sign is positive.

(e) No commas or blanks are allowed within a real constant.

Ex.: +325.34
426.0

-32.76
-48.5792

Real constants can also be expressed as **doubles**. **double** is used when the range of **float** is insufficient. Range of double is is from -1.7e308 to +1.7e308.

Rules for Constructing Character Constants

(a) A character constant is a *single* alphabet, a single digit or a single special symbol enclosed within single inverted commas.

(b) Both the inverted commas should point to the left. For example, 'A' is a valid character constant whereas 'A' is not.

Ex.: 'A'
'I'
'5'
'='

Types of C Variables

A particular type of variable can hold only the same type of constant. For example, an integer variable can hold only an integer constant, a real variable can hold only a real constant and a character variable can hold only a character constant. The rules for constructing different types of constants are different. However, for constructing variable names of all types, the same set of rules applies. These rules are given below.

Rules for Constructing Variable Names

(a) A variable name is any combination of 1 to 31 alphabets, digits or underscores. Some compilers allow variable names whose length could be up to 247 characters. Still, it would be safer to stick to the rule of 31 characters. Do not create unnecessarily long variable names as it adds to your typing effort.

(b) The first character in the variable name must be an alphabet or underscore (_).

(c) No commas or blanks are allowed within a variable name.

(d) No special symbol other than an underscore (as in **gross_sal**) can be used in a variable name.

Ex.: si_int
pop_e_89

Since, the maximum allowable length of a variable name is 31 characters, an enormous number of variable names can be constructed using the above-mentioned rules. It is a good practice to exploit this abundant choice in naming variables by using meaningful variable names.

Thus, if we want to calculate simple interest, it is always advisable to construct meaningful variable names like **prin**, **roi**, **noy** to represent Principle, Rate of interest and Number of years rather than using the variables **a, b, c**.

The rules for creating variable names remain same for all the types of primary and secondary variables. Naturally, the question follows... how is C able to differentiate between these variables? This is a rather simple matter. C compiler is able to distinguish between the variable names by making it compulsory for you to declare the type of any variable name that you wish to use in a program. This type declaration is done at the beginning of the program. Examples of type declaration statements are given below.

```
Ex.:  int  si, m_hra ;
      float  bassal ;
      char  code ;
```

C Keywords

Keywords are the words whose meaning has already been explained to the C compiler (or in a broad sense to the computer). There are only 32 keywords available in C. Figure 2.5 gives a list of these keywords for your ready reference. A detailed discussion of each of these keywords would be taken up in later chapters wherever their use is relevant.

auto	double	int	struct
break	else	long	switch
case	enum	register	typedef
char	extern	return	union
const	float	short	unsigned
continue	for	signed	void
default	goto	sizeof	volatile
do	if	static	while

Figure 2.5

The keywords **cannot** be used as variable names because if we do so, we are trying to assign a new meaning to the keyword, which is not allowed. Some C compilers allow you to construct variable names that exactly resemble the keywords. However, it would be safer not to mix up the variable names and the keywords.

The First C Program

Once armed with the knowledge of variables, constants & keywords, the next logical step would be to combine them to form instructions. However, instead of this, we would write our first C program now. Once we have done that we would see in detail the instructions that it made use of. The first program is very simple. It calculates simple interest for a set of values representing principal, number of years and rate of interest.

```c
/* Calculation of simple interest */
/* Author: gekay  Date: 25/07/2017 */
# include <stdio.h>

int main( )
{
    int  p, n ;
    float  r, si ;

    p = 1000 ;
    n = 3 ;
    r = 8.5 ;

    /* formula for simple interest */
    si = p * n * r / 100 ;

    printf ( "%f\n" , si ) ;
    return 0 ;
}
```

Let us now understand this program in detail.

Form of a C Program

Form of a C program indicates how it has to be written/typed. There are certain rules about the form of a C program that are applicable to all C programs. These are as under:

(a) Each instruction in a C program is written as a separate statement.

(b) The statements in a program must appear in the same order in which we wish them to be executed.

(c) Blank spaces may be inserted between two words to improve the readability of the statement.

(d) All statements should be in lower case letters.

(e) C has no specific rules for the position at which a statement is to be written in a given line. That's why it is often called a free-form language.

(f) Every C statement must end with a semicolon (;). Thus ; acts as a statement terminator.

(g) Comments are used in a C program to clarify either the purpose of the program or the purpose of some statement in the program. Comment about the program should be enclosed within /* */.

What is *main( )*?

main( ) forms a crucial part of any C program. Let us understand its purpose as well as its intricacies.

(a) **main( )** is a function. A function is nothing but a container for a set of statements. In a C program there can be multiple functions. To begin with, we would concentrate only on those programs which have only one function. The name of this function has to be **main( )**, it cannot be anything else. All statements that belong to **main( )** are enclosed within a pair of braces { } as shown below.

```
int main( )
{
    statement 1 ;
    statement 2 ;
    statement 3 ;
}
```

(b) The way functions in a calculator return a value, similarly, functions in C also return a value. **main( )** function always returns an integer value, hence there is an **int** before **main( )**. The integer value that we are returning is 0. 0 indicates success. If for any reason the statements in **main( )** fail to do their intended work we can return a non-zero number from **main( )**. This would indicate failure.

Variables and their Usage

We have learnt constants and variables in isolation. Let us understand their significance with reference to our first C program.

(a) Any variable used in the program must be declared before using it. For example,

```
int  p, n ;             /* declaration */
float  r, si ;          /* declaration */
si = p * n * r / 100 ;  /* usage */
```

(b) In the statement,

```
si = p * n * r / 100 ;
```

* and **/** are the arithmetic operators. The arithmetic operators available in C are **+, -, *** and **/**. C is very rich in operators. There are as many as 45 operators available in C.

Surprisingly there is no operator for exponentiation... a slip, which can be forgiven considering the fact that C has been developed by an individual, not by a committee.

printf( ) and its Purpose

C does not contain any instruction to display output on the screen. All output to screen is achieved using readymade library functions. One such function is **printf( )**. Let us understand this function with respect to our program.

(a) Once the value of **si** is calculated it needs to be displayed on the screen. We have used **printf( )** to do so.

(b) For us to be able to use the **printf( )** function, it is necessary to use **#include <stdio.h>** at the beginning of the program. **#include** is a preprocessor directive. Its purpose will be clarified in Chapter 8. For now, use it whenever you use **printf( )**.

(c) The general form of **printf( )** function is,

```
printf ( "<format string>", <list of variables> ) ;
```

<format string> can contain,

%f for printing real values

%d for printing integer values

%c for printing character values

In addition to format specifiers like **%f, %d** and **%c**, the format string may also contain any other characters. These characters are printed as they are when **printf( )** is executed.

(d) Given below are some more examples of usage of **printf( )** function:

```
printf ( "%f", si ) ;
printf ( "%d %d %f %f", p, n, r, si ) ;
printf ( "Simple interest = Rs. %f", si ) ;
printf ( "Principal = %d \nRate = %f", p, r ) ;
```

The output of the last statement would look like this...

Principal = 1000

Rate = 8.500000

What is '\n' doing in this statement? It is called newline and it takes the cursor to the next line. Therefore, you get the output split over two lines.

(e) **printf( )** can not only print values of variables, it can also print the result of an expression. An expression is nothing but a valid combination of constants, variables and operators. Thus, 3, 3 + 2, c and a + b * c − d all are valid expressions. The results of these expressions can be printed as shown below.

```
printf ( "%d %d %d %d", 3, 3 + 2, c, a + b * c − d ) ;
```

Note that **3** and **c** also represent valid expressions.

Compilation and Execution

Once you have written the program you need to type it and instruct the machine to execute it. To type your C program you need another program called Editor. Once the program has been typed, it needs to be converted to machine language instructions before the machine can execute it. To carry out this conversion we need another program called Compiler. Compiler vendors provide an Integrated Development Environment (IDE) which consists of an Editor as well as the Compiler.

There are several IDEs available in the market targeted towards different operating systems and microprocessors. Details of which IDE to use, how to procure, install and use it are given in Appendix A. Please go through this appendix and install the right IDE on your machine before you try rest of the programs in this book.

Receiving Input

In the program discussed above we assumed the values of **p**, **n** and **r** to be 1000, 3 and 8.5. Every time we run the program we would get the same value for simple interest. If we want to calculate simple interest for some other set of values then we are required to make the relevant changes in the program, and again compile and execute it. Thus the program is not general enough to calculate simple interest for any set of values without being required to make a change in the program. Moreover, if you distribute the EXE file of this program to somebody he would not even be able to make changes in the program. Hence it is a good practice to create a program that is general enough to work for any set of values.

To make the program general, the program itself should ask the user to supply the values of **p**, **n** and **r** through the keyboard during execution. This can be achieved using a function called **scanf( )**. This function is a counter-part of the **printf( )** function. **printf( )** outputs the values to the screen whereas **scanf( )** receives them from the keyboard. This is illustrated in the program given below.

```
/* Calculation of simple interest */
/* Author gekay Date 25/07/2017 */
# include <stdio.h>
int main( )
{
    int   p, n ;
    float  r, si ;

    printf ( "Enter values of p, n, r" ) ;
    scanf ( "%d %d %f", &p, &n, &r ) ;

    si = p * n * r / 100 ;
    printf ( "%f\n" , si ) ;
    return 0 ;
}
```

The first **printf( )** outputs the message 'Enter values of p, n, r' on the screen. Here we have not used any expression in **printf( )** which means that using expressions in **printf( )** is optional.

Note the use of ampersand (**&**) before the variables in the **scanf( )** function is a must. **&** is an 'Address of' operator. It gives the location number (address) used by the variable in memory. When we say **&a**, we are telling **scanf( )** at which memory location should it store the value supplied by the user from the keyboard. The detailed working of the **&** operator would be taken up in Chapter 6.

Note that a blank, a tab or a new line must separate the values supplied to **scanf( )**. A blank is created using a spacebar, tab using the Tab key and new line using the Enter key. This is shown below.

Ex.: The three values separated by blank:

  1000 5 15.5

Ex.: The three values separated by tab:

  1000 5   15.5

Ex.: The three values separated by newline:

  1000
  5
  15.5

So much for the tips. How about writing another program to give you a feel of things. Here it is...

```
/* Just for fun.  Author: Bozo */
# include <stdio.h>
int main( )
{
    int  num ;
    printf ( "Enter a number" ) ;
    scanf ( "%d", &num ) ;

    printf ( "Now I am letting you on a secret...\n" ) ;
    printf ( "You have just entered the number %d\n", num ) ;
    return 0 ;
}
```

Arithmetic Instruction

A C arithmetic instruction consists of a variable name on the left hand side of = and variable names and constants on the right hand side of =. The variables and constants appearing on the right hand side of = are connected by arithmetic operators like +, -, *, and /.

Ex.:   int ad ;
       float kot, deta, alpha, beta, gamma ;
       ad = 3200 ;
       kot = 0.0056 ;
       deta = alpha * beta / gamma + 3.2 * 2 / 5 ;

Here,

   *, /, -, + are the arithmetic operators.

   = is the assignment operator.

   2, 5 and 3200 are integer constants.

   3.2 and 0.0056 are real constants.

   ad is an integer variable.

   kot, deta, alpha, beta, gamma are real variables.

The variables and constants together are called 'operands'. While executing an arithmetic statement the operands on right hand side are operated upon by the 'arithmetic operators' and the result is then assigned, using the assignment operator, to the variable on left-hand side.

A C arithmetic statement could be of three types. These are as follows:

(a) Integer mode arithmetic statement – In this statement all operands are either integer variables or integer constants.

   Ex.: int i, king, issac, noteit ;
         i = i + 1 ;
         king = issac * 234 + noteit - 7689 ;

(b) Real mode arithmetic statement – In this statement all operands are either real constants or real variables.

   Ex.: float qbee, antink, si, prin, anoy, roi ;
         qbee = antink + 23.123 / 4.5 * 0.3442 ;

si = prin * anoy * roi / 100.0 ;

(c) Mixed mode arithmetic statement – In this statement some operands are integers and some operands are real.

Ex.: float si, prin, anoy, roi, avg ;
int a, b, c, num ;
si = prin * anoy * roi / 100.0 ;
avg = (a + b + c + num) / 4 ;

Though Arithmetic instructions look simple to use, one often commits mistakes in writing them. Let us take a closer look at these statements. Note the following points carefully:

(a) C allows only one variable on left-hand side of =. That is, **z = k * l** is legal, whereas **k * l = z** is illegal.

(b) In addition to the division operator C also provides a modular **division** operator. This operator returns the remainder on dividing one integer with another. Thus the expression 10 / 2 yields 5, whereas, 10 % 2 yields 0. Note that the modulus operator (**%**) cannot be applied on a float. Also note that on using % the sign of the remainder is always same as the sign of the numerator. Thus -5 % 2 yields –1, whereas, 5 % -2 yields 1.

(c) An arithmetic instruction is at times used for storing character **constants** in character variables.

char a, b, d ;
a = 'F' ;
b = 'G' ;
d = '+' ;

When we do this, the ASCII values of the characters are stored in the variables. ASCII codes are used to represent any character in memory. For example, ASCII codes of 'F' and 'G' are 01000110 and 01000111. ASCII values are nothing but the decimal equivalent of ASCII codes. Thus ASCII values of 'F' and 'G' are 70 and 71.

(d) **Arithmetic** operations can be performed on **int**s, **float**s and **char**s. Thus the statements,

```
char  x, y ;
int  z ;
x = 'a' ;
y = 'b' ;
z = x + y ;
```

are perfectly valid, since the addition is performed on the ASCII values of the characters and not on characters themselves. The ASCII values of 'a' and 'b' are 97 and 98, and hence can definitely be added.

(e) No operator is assumed to be present. It must be written explicitly. In the following example, the multiplication operator after b must be explicitly written.

```
a = c.d.b(xy)              usual arithmetic statement
a = c * d * b * ( x * y )        C statement
```

(f) There is no operator in C to perform exponentiation operation. Exponentiation has to be carried out as shown below:

```
# include <math.h>
# include <stdio.h>
int main( )
{
    float a ;
    a = pow ( 3.0, 2.0 ) ;
    printf ( "%f", a ) ;
}
```

Here **pow( )** function is a standard library function. It is being used to raise 3.0 to the power of 2.0. The **pow( )** function works only with real numbers, hence we have used 3.0 and 2.0 instead of 3 and 2.

#include <math.h> is a preprocessor directive. It is being used here to ensure that the **pow( )** function works correctly. You can explore other mathematical functions like **abs( )**, **sqrt( )**, **sin( )**, **cos( )**, **tan( )**, etc., declared in **math.h** on your own.

Integer and Float Conversions

In order to effectively develop C programs, it will be necessary to understand the rules that are used for the implicit conversion of floating point and integer values in C. These are mentioned below. Note them carefully.

(g) An arithmetic operation between an integer and integer always yields an integer result.

(h) An operation between a real and real always yields a real result.

(i) An operation between an integer and real always yields a real result. In this operation the integer is first promoted to a real and then the operation is performed. Hence the result is real.

I think a few practical examples shown in Figure 2.6 would put the issue beyond doubt.

Operation	Result	Operation	Result
5 / 2	2	2 / 5	0
5.0 / 2	2.5	2.0 / 5	0.4
5 / 2.0	2.5	2 / 5.0	0.4
5.0 / 2.0	2.5	2.0 / 5.0	0.4

Figure 2.6

Type Conversion in Assignments

It may so happen that the type of the expression on right hand side and the type of the variable on the left-hand side of an assignment operator may not be same. In such a case, the value of the expression is promoted or demoted depending on the type of the variable on left-hand side of =.

For example, consider the following assignment statements.

```
int  i ;
float  b ;
i = 3.5 ;
b = 30 ;
```

Here in the first assignment statement, though the expression's value is a **float** (3.5), it cannot be stored in **i** since it is an **int**. In such a case, the **float** is demoted to an **int** and then its value is stored. Hence what gets stored in **i** is 3. Exactly opposite happens in the next statement. Here, 30 is promoted to 30.0 and then stored in **b**, since **b** being a **float** variable cannot hold anything except a **float** value.

Instead of a simple expression used in the above examples, if a complex expression occurs, still the same rules apply. For example, consider the following program fragment.

float a, b, c ; int s ;
s = a * b * c / 100 + 32 / 4 - 3 * 1.1 ;

Here, in the assignment statement, some operands are **int**s whereas others are **float**s. As we know, during evaluation of the expression, the **int**s would be promoted to **float**s and the result of the expression would be a **float**. But when this **float** value is assigned to **s** it is again demoted to an **int** and then stored in **s**.

Observe the results of the arithmetic statements shown in Figure 2.7. It has been assumed that **k** is an integer variable and **a** is a real variable.

Arithmetic Instruction	Result	Arithmetic Instruction	Result
k = 2 / 9	0	a = 2 / 9	0.0
k = 2.0 / 9	0	a = 2.0 / 9	0.222222
k = 2 / 9.0	0	a = 2 / 9.0	0.222222
k = 2.0 / 9.0	0	a = 2.0 / 9.0	0.222222
k = 9 / 2	4	a = 9 / 2	4.0
k = 9.0 / 2	4	a = 9.0 / 2	4.5
k = 9 / 2.0	4	a = 9 / 2.0	4.5
k = 9.0 / 2.0	4	a = 9.0 / 2.0	4.5

Figure 2.7

Note that though the following statements give the same result, 0, the results are obtained differently.

k = 2 / 9 ;
k = 2.0 / 9 ;

In the first statement, since both 2 and 9 are integers, the result is an integer, i.e. 0. This 0 is then assigned to **k**. In the second statement 9 is promoted to 9.0 and then the division is performed. Division yields 0.222222. However, this cannot be stored in **k**, **k** being an **int**. Hence it gets demoted to 0 and then stored in **k**.

More Operators

Apart from arithmetic operators, C language provides many other operators which can be classified into categories shown in Figure 2.8.

Increment / Decrement	++, --
Compound Assignment	+=, -=, *=, /=, %=
Relational operators	<, >, <=, >=, ==, !=
Logical operators	&&, ||, !
Bitwise operators	~, <<, >>, &, |, ^

Figure 2.8

Of these the **++** and **--** operators are used to increment or decrement the value of a variable by 1. Thus the expression **i++** is same as **i = i + 1**. Likewise, **i--** is same as **i = i - 1**.

The compound assignment operators can increment or decrement a variable by any value. Thus **a = a + 0.5** is same as **a += 0.5**. Likewise, **b = b / 12** is same as **b /= 12**.

The relational operators are used to test the relationship between two entities. For example, the condition **a < b** checks whether value of **a** is less than that of **b**. The logical operators are used to combine multiple conditions or to negate the result of a condition. Both these types of operators are discussed in detail in Unit 3.

The bitwise operators are to manipulate individual bits of a byte.

Hierarchy of Operations

While executing an arithmetic statement that has multiple operators, there might be some issues about their evaluation. For example, does the expression 2 * x - 3 * y correspond to (2x)-(3y) or to 2(x-3y)? Similarly, does A / B * C correspond to A / (B * C) or to (A / B) * C? To answer these questions satisfactorily, one has to understand the 'hierarchy' of operations. The priority or precedence in which the operations in an arithmetic statement are performed is called the hierarchy of operations. The hierarchy of commonly used operators is shown in Figure 2.9.

Priority	Operators	Description
1st	* / %	Multiplication, Division, Modular division
2nd	+ -	Addition, Subtraction
3rd	=	Assignment

Figure 2.9

Now a few tips about usage of operators in general.

(a) Within parentheses the same hierarchy as mentioned in Figure 2.9 is operative. Also, if there are more than one set of parentheses, the operations within the innermost parentheses would be performed first, followed by the operations within the second innermost pair and so on.

(b) We must always remember to use pairs of parentheses. A careless imbalance of the right and left parentheses is a common error. Best way to avoid this error is to type ( ) and then type an expression inside it.

A few examples would clarify the issue further.

Example 2.1: Determine the hierarchy of operations and evaluate the following expression, assuming that **i** is an integer variable:

i = 2 * 3 / 4 + 4 / 4 + 8 - 2 + 5 / 8

Stepwise evaluation of this expression is shown below:

```
i = 2 * 3 / 4 + 4 / 4 + 8 - 2 + 5 / 8
i = 6 / 4 + 4 / 4 + 8 - 2 + 5 / 8          operation: *
i = 1 + 4 / 4 + 8 - 2 + 5 / 8              operation: /
i = 1 + 1+ 8 - 2 + 5 / 8                   operation: /
i = 1 + 1 + 8 - 2 + 0                      operation: /
i = 2 + 8 - 2 + 0                          operation: +
i = 10 - 2 + 0                             operation: +
i = 8 + 0                                  operation : -
i = 8                                      operation: +
```

Note that 6 / 4 gives 1 and not 1.5. This so happens because 6 and 4 both are integers and therefore 6 / 4 must evaluate to an integer. Similarly 5 / 8 evaluates to zero, since 5 and 8 are integers and hence 5 / 8 must return an integer value.

Example 2.2: Determine the hierarchy of operations and evaluate the following expression, assuming that **kk** is a float variable:

kk = 3 / 2 * 4 + 3 / 8

Stepwise evaluation of this expression is shown below:

kk = 3 / 2 * 4 + 3 / 8	
kk = 1 * 4 + 3 / 8	operation: /
kk = 4 + 3 / 8	operation: *
kk = 4 + 0	operation: /
kk = 4	operation: +

Note that 3 / 8 gives zero, again for the same reason mentioned in the previous example.

Associativity of Operators

When an expression contains two operators of equal priority the tie between them is settled using the associativity of the operators. All operators in C have either Left to Right associativity or Right to Left associativity. Let us understand this with the help of a few examples.

Consider the expression a = 3 / 2 * 5 ;

Here there is a tie between operators of same priority, that is between / and *. This tie is settled using the associativity of / and *. Both enjoy Left to Right associativity. Therefore firstly / operation is done followed by *.

Consider one more expression.

a = b = 3 ;

Here both assignment operators have the same priority. So order of operations is decided using associativity of = operator. = associates from Right to Left. Therefore, second = is performed earlier than first =.

Consider yet another expression.

z = a * b + c / d ;

Here * and / enjoys same priority and same associativity (Left to Right). Compiler is free to perform * or / operation as per its convenience, since no matter which is performed earlier, the result would be same.

Appendix B gives the associativity of all the operators available in C. Note that the precedence and associativity of all operators is predetermined and we cannot change it.

Storage Classes in C

We have already said all that needs to be said about constants, but we are not finished with variables. To fully define a variable, one needs to mention not only its 'type' but also its 'storage class'. In other words, not only do all variables have a data type, they also have a 'storage class'.

We have not mentioned storage classes yet, though we have written several programs in C. We were able to get away with this because storage classes have defaults. If we don't specify the storage class of a variable in its declaration, the compiler will assume a storage class depending on the context in which the variable is used. Thus, variables have certain default storage classes.

From C compiler's point of view, a variable name identifies some physical location within the computer where the string of bits representing the variable's value is stored. There are basically two kinds of locations in a computer where such a value may be kept— Memory and CPU registers. It is the variable's storage class that determines in which of these two types of locations, the value is stored.

Moreover, a variable's storage class tells us:

(a)   Where the variable would be stored.

(b)   What will be the initial value of the variable, if initial value is not specifically assigned.(i.e. the default initial value).

(c)   What is the scope of the variable; i.e. in which functions the value of the variable would be available.

(d)   What is the life of the variable; i.e. how long would the variable exist.

There are four storage classes in C:

(a)   Automatic storage class
(b)   Register storage class

(c)   Static storage class

(d)   External storage class

Let us examine these storage classes one by one.

Automatic Storage Class

The features of a variable defined to have an automatic storage class are as under:

Storage: Memory.

Default value: An unpredictable value, often called a garbage value.

Scope: Local to the block in which the variable is defined.

Life: Till the control remains within the block in which the variable is defined.

Following program shows how an automatic storage class variable is declared, and the fact that if the variable is not initialized, it contains a garbage value.

```
# include <stdio.h>
int main( )
{
    auto int  i, j ;
    printf ( "%d  %d\n", i, j ) ;
    return 0 ;
}
```

The output of the above program could be...

1211 221

where, 1211 and 221 are garbage values of **i** and **j**. When you run this program, you may get different values, since garbage values are unpredictable. So always make it a point that you initialize the automatic variables properly, otherwise you are likely to get unexpected results. Note that the keyword for this storage class is **auto**, and not automatic.

Scope and life of an automatic variable is illustrated in the following program.

```
# include <stdio.h>
int main( )
{
```

```
   auto int  i = 1 ;
   {
       auto int  i = 2 ;
       {
           auto int  i = 3 ;
           printf ( "%d ", i ) ;
       }
       printf ( "%d ", i ) ;
   }
   printf ( "%d\n", i ) ;
   return 0 ;
}
```

The output of the above program would be:

3 2 1

Note that the Compiler treats the three **i**'s as totally different variables, since they are defined in different blocks. All three **i**'s are available to the innermost **printf( )**. This is because the innermost **printf( )** lies in all the three blocks (a block is all statements enclosed within a pair of braces) in which the three **i**'s are defined. This **printf( )** prints 3 because when all three **i**'s are available, the one which is most local (nearest to **printf( )**) is given a priority.

Once the control comes out of the innermost block, the variable **i** with value 3 is lost, and hence the **i** in the second **printf( )** refers to **i** with value 2. Similarly, when the control comes out of the next innermost block, the third **printf( )** refers to the **i** with value 1.

Register Storage Class

The features of a variable defined to be of **register** storage class are as under:

Storage: CPU registers.
Default value: Garbage value.
Scope: Local to the block in which the variable is defined.
Life: Till the control remains within the block in which the variable is defined.

A value stored in a CPU register can always be accessed faster than the one that is stored in memory. Therefore, if a variable is used at many places in a program, it is better to declare its storage class as **register**. A good example of frequently used variables is loop counters. We can name their storage class as **register**.

```
# include <stdio.h>
int main( )
{
    register int  i ;

    for ( i = 1 ; i <= 10 ; i++ )
        printf ( "%d\n", i ) ;
    return 0 ;
}
```

Here, even though we have declared the storage class of **i** as **register**, we cannot say for sure that the value of **i** would be stored in a CPU register. Why? Because the number of CPU registers are limited, and they may be busy doing some other task. What happens in such an event... the variable works as if its storage class is **auto**.

Static Storage Class

The features of a variable defined to have a **static** storage class are as under:

Storage:	Memory.
Default value:	Zero.
Scope:	Local to the block in which the variable is defined.
Life:	Value of the variable persists between different function calls.

Compare the two programs and their output given in Figure 2.10 to understand the difference between the **automatic** and **static** storage classes.

The programs in Figure 2.10 consist of two functions **main( )** and **increment( )**. The function **increment( )** gets called from **main( )** thrice. Each time it prints the value of **i** and then increments it. The only difference in the two programs is that one uses an **auto** storage class for variable **i**, whereas the other uses **static** storage class.

```
#include <stdio.h>                  #include <stdio.h>
void increment( ) ;                 void increment( ) ;
int main( )                         int main( )
{                                   {
    increment( ) ;                      increment( ) ;
    increment( ) ;                      increment( ) ;
    increment( ) ;                      increment( ) ;
    return 0 ;                          return 0 ;
}                                   }
void increment( )                   void increment( )
{                                   {
    auto int i = 1 ;                    static int i = 1 ;
    printf ( "%d\n", i ) ;              printf ( "%d\n", i ) ;
    i = i + 1 ;                         i = i + 1 ;
}                                   }
```

The output of the above programs would be:

```
          1                                  1
          1                                  2
          1                                  3
```

Figure 2.10

Like **auto** variables, **static** variables are also local to the block in which they are declared. The difference between them is that **static** variables don't disappear when the function is no longer active. Their values persist. If the control comes back to the same function again, the **static** variables have the same values they had last time around.

In the above example, when variable **i** is **auto**, each time **increment( )** is called, it is re-initialized to one. When the function terminates, **i** vanishes and its new value of 2 is lost. The result: no matter how many times we call **increment( ), i** is initialized to 1 every time.

On the other hand, if **i** is **static**, it is initialized to 1 only once. It is never initialized again. During the first call to **increment( )**, **i** is incremented to 2. Because **i** is static, this value persists. The next time **increment( )** is called, **i** is not re-initialized to 1; on the contrary, its old value 2 is still available. This current value of **i** (i.e. 2) gets printed and then **i = i + 1** adds 1 to **i** to get a value of 3. When **increment( )** is called the third time, the current value of **i** (i.e. 3) gets printed and once again **i** is incremented. In short, if the storage class is **static**, then the statement **static int i = 1** is executed only once, irrespective of how many times the same function is called.

External Storage Class

The features of a variable whose storage class has been defined as external are as follows:

Storage: Memory.
Default value: Zero.
Scope: Global.
Life: As long as the program's execution doesn't come to an end.

External variables differ from those we have already discussed in that their scope is global, not local. External variables are declared outside all functions, yet are available to all functions that care to use them. Here is an example to illustrate this fact.

```
# include <stdio.h>

int  i ;
void increment( ) ;
void decrement( ) ;

int main( )
{
    printf ( "\ni = %d", i ) ;
    increment( ) ;
    increment( ) ;
    decrement( ) ;
    decrement( ) ;
    return 0 ;
}
void increment( )
{
    i = i + 1 ;
    printf ( "on incrementing i = %d\n", i ) ;
}
void decrement( )
{
    i = i - 1 ;
    printf ( "on decrementing i = %d\n", i ) ;
}
```

The output would be:

i = 0
on incrementing i = 1
on incrementing i = 2
on decrementing i = 1
on decrementing i = 0

As is obvious from the above output, the value of **i** is available to the functions **increment( )** and **decrement( )** since **i** has been declared outside all functions.

Exercise

[A] Which of the following are invalid C constants and why?

'3.15'	35,550	3.25e2
2e-3	'eLearning'	"show"
'Quest'	2^3	4 6 5 2

[B] Which of the following are invalid variable names and why?

B'day	int	$hello
#HASH	dot.	number
totalArea	_main( )	temp_in_Deg

[C] State whether the following statements are True or False:

(a) C language has been developed by Dennis Ritchie.

(b) Operating systems like Windows, UNIX, Linux and Android are written in C.

(c) C language programs can easily interact with hardware of a PC / Laptop.

(d) A real constant in C can be expressed in both Fractional and Exponential forms.

(e) A character variable can at a time store only one character.

(f) The maximum value that an integer constant can have varies from one compiler to another.

(g) Usually all C statements are written in small case letters.

(h) Spaces may be inserted between two words in a C statement.

(i) Spaces cannot be present within a variable name.

(j) C programs are converted into machine language with the help of a program called Editor.

(k) Most development environments provide an Editor to type a C program and a Compiler to convert it into machine language.

(l) int, char, float, real, integer, character, char, main, printf and scanf all are keywords.

[D] Match the following:

(a)	\n	Literal
(b)	3.145	Statement terminator
(c)	-6513	Character constant

(d)	'D'	Escape sequence
(e)	4.25e-3	Input function
(f)	main( )	Function
(g)	%f, %d, %c	Integer constant
(h)	;	Address of operator
(i)	Constant	Output function
(j)	Variable	Format specifier
(k)	&	Exponential form
(l)	printf( )	Real constant
(m)	scanf( )	Identifier

[E] Evaluate the following expressions and show their hierarchy.

(a) ans = 5 * b * b * x - 3 * a * y * y - 8 * b * b * x + 10 * a * y ;

(a = 3, b = 2, x = 5, y = 4 assume **ans** to be an int)

(b) res = 4 * a * y / c - a * y / c ;

(a = 4, y = 1, c = 3, assume **res** to be an int)

(c) s = c + a * y * y / b ;

(a = 2.2, b = 0.0, c = 4.1, y = 3.0, assume **s** to be an float)

(d) R = x * x + 2 * x + 1 / 2 * x * x + x + 1 ;

(x = 3.5, assume **R** to be an float)

[F] Indicate the order in which the following expressions would be evaluated:

(a) g = 10 / 5 / 2 / 1 ;

(b) b = 3 / 2 + 5 * 4 / 3 ;

(c) a = b = c = 3 + 4 ;

(d) x = 2 − 3 + 5 * 2 / 8 % 3 ;

(e) z = 5 % 3 / 8 * 3 + 4

(f) y = z = -3 % -8 / 2 + 7 ;

[G] What will be the output of the following programs:

(a)
```
# include <stdio.h>
int main( )
{
    int  i = 2, j = 3, k, l ;
    float   a, b ;
```

```
        k = i / j * j ;
        l = j / i * i ;
        a = i / j * j ;
        b = j / i * i ;
        printf ( "%d %d %f %f\n", k, l, a, b ) ;
        return 0 ;
    }
```

(b) # include <stdio.h>
```
    int main( )
    {
        int  a, b, c, d ;
        a = 2 % 5 ;
        b = -2 % 5 ;
        c = 2 % -5 ;
        d = -2 % -5 ;
        printf ( "a = %d b = %d c = %d d = %d\n", a, b, c, d ) ;
        return 0 ;
    }
```

(c) # include <stdio.h>
```
    int main( )
    {
        float a = 5,  b = 2 ;
        int c, d ;
        c = a % b ;
        d = a / 2 ;
        printf ( "%d\n", d ) ;
        return 0 ;
    }
```

[H] Point out the errors, if any, in the following programs:

(a) int main( )
```
    {
        int a, float b, int c ;
        a = 25 ; b = 3.24 ; c = a + b * b – 35 ;
    }
```

(b) /* Calculation of average
```
        /* Author: Sanjay */
        /* Place – Whispering Bytes */
    */
```

```
#include <stdio.h>
int main( )
{
    int  a = 35 ; float b = 3.24 ;
    printf ( "%d %f %d", a, b + 1.5, 235 ) ;
}
```

(c)
```
#include <stdio.h>
int main( )
{
    int  a, b, c ;
    scanf ( "%d %d %d", a, b, c ) ;
}
```

(d)
```
#include <stdio.h>
int main( )
{
    int  m1, m2, m3
    printf ( "Enter values of marks in 3 subjects" )
    scanf ( "%d %d %d", &m1, &m2, &m3 )
    printf ( "You entered %d %d %d", m1, m2, m3 ) ;
}
```

[I] Point out the errors, if any, in the following C statements:

(e) x = (y + 3) ;

(f) cir = 2 * 3.141593 * r ;

(g) char = '3' ;

(h) 4 / 3 * 3.14 * r * r * r = vol_of_sphere ;

(i) volume = a^3 ;

(j) area = 1 / 2 * base * height ;

(k) si = p * r * n / 100 ;

(l) area of circle = 3.14 * r * r ;

(m) peri_of_tri = a + b + c ;

(n) slope = (y2 – y1) ÷ (x2 – x1) ;

[J] Attempt the following:

(a) Ramesh's basic salary is input through the keyboard. His dearness allowance is 40% of basic salary, and house rent allowance is 20% of basic salary. Write a program to calculate his gross salary.

(b) The distance between two cities (in km.) is input through the keyboard. Write a program to convert and print this distance in meters, feet, inches and centimeters.

(c) If the marks obtained by a student in five different subjects are input through the keyboard, write a program to find out the aggregate marks and percentage marks obtained by the student. Assume that the maximum marks that can be obtained by a student in each subject is 100.

(d) Temperature of a city in Fahrenheit degrees is input through the keyboard. Write a program to convert this temperature into Centigrade degrees.

(e) The length and breadth of a rectangle and radius of a circle are input through the keyboard. Write a program to calculate the area and perimeter of the rectangle, and the area and circumference of the circle.

(o) If a five-digit number is input through the keyboard, write a program to calculate the sum of its digits. (Hint: Use the modulus operator '%')

(p) If a five-digit number is input through the keyboard, write a program to reverse the number.

(q) If lengths of three sides of a triangle are input through the keyboard, write a program to find the area of the triangle.

(r) Write a program to receive Cartesian co-ordinates (x, y) of a point and convert them into polar co-ordinates (r, ▮

Hint: $r = sqrt(x^2 + y^2)$ and ▮▮ $an^{-1} (y / x)$

Unit 3

Conditional Program Execution & Functions

- Decisions! Decisions!
- The *if* Statement
    - Multiple Statements within *if*
- The *if-else* Statement
    - Nested *if-else*s
- Use of Logical Operators
    - The ! Operator
- Decisions using switch
    - Tips and Traps
- Loops
- The while Loop
    - Tips and Traps
- The for Loop
    - Multiple Initializations in the for Loop
- The break Statement
- The continue Statement
- The do-while Loop
- What is a Function?
- Passing Values between Functions
- Return Type of Function
- Recursion
- Exercise

We all need to alter our actions in the face of changing circumstances. If the weather is fine, then I will go for a stroll. If the highway is busy, I would take a diversion. If the pitch takes spin, we would win the match.

C language too must be able to perform different sets of actions depending on the circumstances. C has three major decision making instructions—the **if** statement, the **if-else** statement, and the **switch** statement.

Also, in programming we frequently need to perform an action over and over, often with variations in the details each time. The mechanism, which meets this need, is the 'Loop Control Instruction'. We would be learning decision control instruction and loop control instruction in this unit.

Decisions! Decisions!

In the programs written in Unit 1, we have used sequence control instruction, i.e. the statements in them got executed in the same order in which they appeared in the program. To execute the instructions sequentially, we don't have to do anything at all. That is, by default, the instructions in a program are executed sequentially.

However, in serious programming situations, seldom do we want the instructions to be executed sequentially. Many a time, we want a set of instructions to be executed in one situation, and an entirely different set of instructions to be executed in another situation. This kind of situation is dealt with in C programs using a decision control instruction. As mentioned earlier, a decision control instruction can be implemented in C using:

(a)   The **if** statement
(b)   The **if-else** statement
(c)   The switch statement

Now let us learn each of these and their variations in turn.

The *if* Statement

C uses the keyword **if** to implement the decision control instruction. The general form of if statement looks like this:

if (this condition is true)
        execute this statement ;

The keyword **if** tells the compiler that what follows is a decision control instruction. The condition following the keyword **if** is always enclosed within a pair of parentheses. If the condition, whatever it is, is true, then the statement is executed. If the condition is not true, then the statement is not executed; instead the program skips past it. But how do we express the condition itself in C? And how do we evaluate its truth or falsity? As a general rule, we express a condition using C's 'relational' operators. The relational operators allow us to compare two values to see whether they are equal to each other, unequal, or whether one is greater than the other. Figure 3.1 shows how they look and how they are evaluated in C.

this expression	is true if
x == y	x is equal to y
x != y	x is not equal to y
x < y	x is less than y
x > y	x is greater than y
x <= y	x is less than or equal to y
x >= y	x is greater than or equal to y

Figure 3.1

The relational operators should be familiar to you except for the equality operator == and the inequality operator !=. Note that = is used for assignment, whereas, == is used for comparison of two quantities. Here is a simple program that demonstrates the use of **if** and the relational operators.

```
/* Demonstration of if statement */
# include <stdio.h>
int main( )
{
    int  num ;

    printf ( "Enter a number less than 10 " ) ;
    scanf ( "%d", &num ) ;

    if ( num < 10 )
        printf ( "What an obedient servant you are !\n" ) ;
```

```
        return 0 ;
}
```

On execution of this program, if you type a number less than 10, you get a message on the screen through **printf( )**. If you type some other number the program doesn't do anything. The flowchart given in Figure 3.2 would help you understand the flow of control in the program.

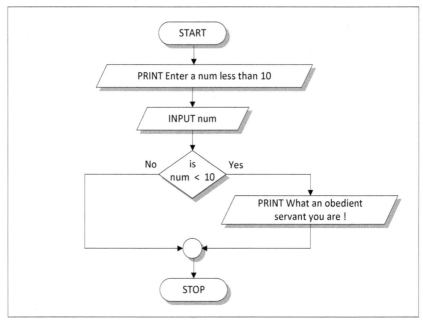

Figure 3.2

To make you comfortable with the decision control instruction, one more example has been given below. Study it carefully before reading further.

Example 3.1: While purchasing certain items, a discount of 10% is offered if the quantity purchased is more than 1000. If quantity and price per item are input through the keyboard, write a program to calculate the total expenses.

```
/* Calculation of total expenses */
# include <stdio.h>
int main( )
{
    int   qty, dis = 0 ;
    float   rate, tot ;
```

```
printf ( "Enter quantity and rate " ) ;
scanf ( "%d %f", &qty, &rate) ;

if ( qty > 1000 )
    dis = 10 ;

tot = ( qty * rate ) - ( qty * rate * dis / 100 ) ;
printf ( "Total expenses = Rs. %f\n", tot ) ;

return 0 ;
}
```

Here is some sample interaction with the program.

```
Enter quantity and rate 1200 15.50
Total expenses = Rs. 16740.000000


Enter quantity and rate 200 15.50
Total expenses = Rs. 3100.000000
```

In the first run of the program, the condition evaluates to true, as 1200 (value of **qty**) is greater than 1000. Therefore, the variable **dis**, which was earlier set to 0, now gets a new value 10. Using this new value, total expenses are calculated and printed.

In the second run, the condition evaluates to false, as 200 (the value of **qty**) isn't greater than 1000. Thus, **dis**, which is earlier set to 0, remains 0, and hence the expression after the minus sign evaluates to zero, thereby offering no discount.

Is the statement **dis = 0** necessary? The answer is yes, since in C, a variable, if not specifically initialized, contains some unpredictable value (garbage value).

Multiple Statements within *if*

It may so happen that in a program we want more than one statement to be executed if the expression following **if** is satisfied. If such multiple statements are to be executed, then they must be placed within a pair of braces, as illustrated in the following example:

Example 3.2: The current year and the year in which the employee joined the organization are entered through the keyboard. If the number of years for which the employee has served the organization is greater than 3, then a bonus of Rs. 2500/- is given to the employee. If the years of service are not greater than 3, then the program should do nothing.

```
/* Calculation of bonus */
# include <stdio.h>
int main( )
{
    int   bonus, cy, yoj, yos ;

    printf ( "Enter current year and year of joining " ) ;
    scanf ( "%d %d", &cy, &yoj ) ;

    yos = cy - yoj ;

    if ( yos > 3 )
    {
        bonus = 2500 ;
        printf ( "Bonus = Rs. %d\n", bonus ) ;
    }

    return 0 ;
}
```

Observe that here the two statements to be executed on satisfaction of the condition have been enclosed within a pair of braces. If a pair of braces is not used, then the C compiler assumes that the programmer wants only the immediately next statement after the **if** to be executed on satisfaction of the condition. In other words, we can say that the default scope of the **if** statement is the immediately next statement after it.

The *if-else* Statement

The **if** statement by itself will execute a single statement, or a group of statements, when the expression following **if** evaluates to true. It does nothing when the expression evaluates to false. Can we execute one group of statements if the expression evaluates to true and another group of statements if the expression evaluates to false? Of course! This is what is the purpose of the **else** statement that is demonstrated in the following example:

Example 3.3: In a company an employee is paid as under:

If his basic salary is less than Rs. 1500, then HRA = 10% of basic salary and DA = 90% of basic salary. If his salary is either equal to or above Rs. 1500, then HRA = Rs. 500 and DA = 98% of basic salary. If the employee's salary is input through the keyboard write a program to find his gross salary.

```c
/* Calculation of gross salary */
# include <stdio.h>
int main( )
{
    float   bs, gs, da, hra ;

    printf ( "Enter basic salary " ) ;
    scanf ( "%f", &bs ) ;

    if ( bs < 1500 )
    {
        hra = bs * 10 / 100 ;
        da = bs * 90 / 100 ;
    }
    else
    {
        hra = 500 ;
        da = bs * 98 / 100 ;
    }
    gs = bs + hra + da ;
    printf ( "gross salary = Rs. %f\n", gs ) ;

    return 0 ;
}
```

Figure 3.3 would help you understand the flow of control in the program.

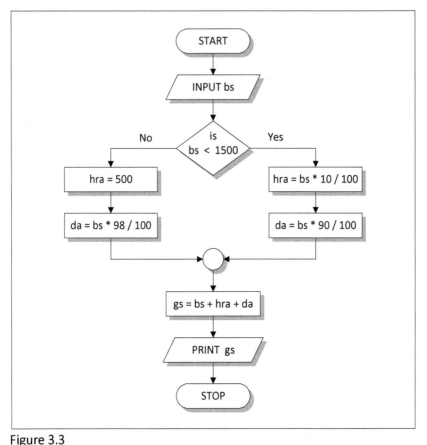

Figure 3.3

A few points worth noting about the program...

(a) The group of statements after the **if** upto and not including the **else** is called an 'if block'. Similarly, the statements after the **else** form the 'else block'.

(b) Notice that the **else** is written exactly below the **if**. The statements in the if block and those in the else block have been indented to the right. This formatting convention is followed throughout the book to enable you to understand the working of the program better.

(c) Had there been only one statement to be executed in the if block and only one statement in the else block we could have dropped the pair of braces.

(d) As with the **if** statement, the default scope of **else** is also the statement immediately after the **else**. To override this default scope, a pair of braces, as shown in the above example, must be used.

Nested *if-elses*

It is perfectly alright if we write an entire **if-else** construct within either the body of the **if** statement or the body of an **else** statement. This is called 'nesting'of **if**s. This is shown in the following program:

```
/* A quick demo of nested if-else */
# include <stdio.h>
int main( )
{
    int  i ;

    printf ( "Enter either 1 or 2 " ) ;
    scanf ( "%d", &i ) ;

    if ( i == 1 )
        printf ( "You would go to heaven !\n" ) ;
    else
    {
        if ( i == 2 )
            printf ( "Hell was created with you in mind\n" ) ;
        else
            printf ( "How about mother earth !\n" ) ;
    }

    return 0 ;
}
```

Note that the second **if-else** construct is nested in the first **else** statement. If the condition in the first **if** statement is false, then the condition in the second **if** statement is checked. If it is false as well, then the final **else** statement is executed.

You can see in the program how each time a **if-else** construct is nested within another **if-else** construct, it is also indented to add clarity to the program.

In the above program, an **if-else** occurs within the 'else block' of the first **if** statement. Similarly, in some other program, an **if-else** may occur in the 'if block' as well. There is no limit on how deeply the ifs and the elses can be nested.

Use of Logical Operators

C allows usage of three logical operators, namely, &&, || and !. These are to be read as 'AND', 'OR' and 'NOT', respectively.

There are several things to note about these logical operators. Most obviously, two of them are composed of double symbols: || and &&.

The first two operators, && and ||, allow two or more conditions to be combined in an if statement. Let us see how they are used in a program. Consider the following example:

Example 3.4: The marks obtained by a student in 5 different subjects are input through the keyboard. The student gets a division as per the following rules:

Percentage above or equal to 60 - First division
Percentage between 50 and 59 - Second division
Percentage between 40 and 49 - Third division
Percentage less than 40 - Fail

Write a program to calculate the division obtained by the student.

There are two ways in which we can write a program for this example. These methods are given below.

```
/* Method – I */
# include <stdio.h>
int main( )
{
    int  m1, m2, m3, m4, m5, per ;

    printf ( "Enter marks in five subjects " ) ;
    scanf ( "%d %d %d %d %d", &m1, &m2, &m3, &m4, &m5 ) ;
    per = ( m1 + m2 + m3 + m4 + m5 ) * 100 / 500 ;

    if ( per >= 60 )
        printf ( "First division\n" ) ;
    else
    {
        if ( per >= 50 )
            printf ( "Second division\n" ) ;
```

```
        else
        {
            if ( per >= 40 )
                printf ( "Third division\n" ) ;
            else
                printf ( "Fail\n" ) ;
        }
    }

    return 0 ;
}
```

This is a straight-forward program. Observe that the program uses nested **if-else**s. Though the program works fine, it has three disadvantages:

(a) As the number of conditions go on increasing the level of indentation also goes on increasing. As a result, the whole program creeps to the right. So much so that entire program is not visible on the screen. So if something goes wrong with the program locating what is wrong where becomes difficult.

(b) Care needs to be exercised to match the corresponding **if**s and **else**s.

(c) Care needs to be exercised to match the corresponding pair of braces.

All these three problems can be eliminated by usage of 'Logical Operators'. The following program illustrates this:

```
/* Method – II */
# include <stdio.h>
int main( )
{
    int  m1, m2, m3, m4, m5, per ;

    printf ( "Enter marks in five subjects " ) ;
    scanf ( "%d %d %d %d %d", &m1, &m2, &m3, &m4, &m5 ) ;

    per = ( m1 + m2 + m3 + m4 + m5 ) / 500 * 100 ;

    if ( per >= 60 )
        printf ( "First division\n" ) ;
```

```
    if ( ( per >= 50 ) && ( per < 60 ) )
        printf ( "Second division\n" ) ;

    if ( ( per >= 40 ) && ( per < 50 ) )
        printf ( "Third division\n" ) ;

    if ( per < 40 )
        printf ( "Fail\n" ) ;

    return 0 ;
}
```

As can be seen from the second **if** statement, the **&&** operator is used to combine two conditions. 'Second division' gets printed if both the conditions evaluate to true. If one of the conditions evaluate to false then the whole thing is treated as false.

The ! Operator

So far we have used only the logical operators **&&** and **||**. The third logical operator is the NOT operator, written as **!**. This operator reverses the result of the expression it operates on. For example, if the expression evaluates to a non-zero value, then applying **!** operator to it results into a 0. Vice versa, if the expression evaluates to zero then on applying **!** operator to it makes it 1, a non-zero value. The final result (after applying **!**) 0 or 1 is considered to be false or true, respectively. Here is an example of the NOT operator applied to a relational expression.

!(y < 10)

This means 'not **y** less than 10'. In other words, if **y** is less than 10, the expression will be false, since **(y < 10)** is true. We can express the same condition as **(y >= 10)**.

The NOT operator is often used to reverse the logical value of a single variable, as in the expression

if (! flag)

This is another way of saying:

if (flag == 0)

Does the NOT operator sound confusing? Avoid it if you want, as the same thing can be achieved without using the NOT operator.

Decisions using *switch*

Often while programming the choice that we are required to make is more complicated than merely selecting between two alternatives. C provides a special control statement that allows us to handle such cases effectively; rather than using a series of **if** statements.

The control statement that allows us to make a decision from the number of choices is called a **switch**, or more correctly a **switch-case-default**, since these three keywords go together to make up the control statement. They most often appear as follows:

```
switch ( integer expression )
{
    case constant 1 :
        do this ;
    case constant 2 :
        do this ;
    case constant 3 :
        do this ;
    default :
        do this ;
}
```

The integer expression following the keyword **switch** is any C expression that will yield an integer value. It could be an integer constant like 1, 2 or 3, or an expression that evaluates to an integer. The keyword **case** is followed by an integer or a character constant. Each constant in each **case** must be different from all the others. The "do this" lines in the above form of **switch** represent any valid C statement.

What happens when we run a program containing a **switch**? First, the integer expression following the keyword **switch** is evaluated. The value it gives is then matched, one-by-one, against the constant values that follow the **case** statements. When a match is found, the program executes the statements following that **case**, and all subsequent **case** and **default** statements as well. If no match is found with any of the **case** statements, only the statements following the **default** case are executed. A few examples will show how this control instruction works.

Consider the following program:

```
# include <stdio.h>
int main( )
{
    int  i = 2 ;

    switch ( i )
    {
        case 1 :
            printf ( "I am in case 1 \n" ) ;
        case 2 :
            printf ( "I am in case 2 \n" ) ;
        case 3 :
            printf ( "I am in case 3 \n" ) ;
        default :
            printf ( "I am in default \n" ) ;
    }
    return 0 ;
}
```

The output of this program would be:

I am in case 2
I am in case 3
I am in default

The output is definitely not what we expected! We didn't expect the second and third line in the above output. The program prints case 2 and case 3 and the default case. Well, yes. We said the **switch** executes the case where a match is found and all the subsequent **case**s and the **default** as well.

If you want that only case 2 should get executed, it is up to you to get out of the **switch** then and there by using a **break** statement. The following example shows how this is done. Note that there is no need for a **break** statement after the **default**, since on reaching the **default** case, the control comes out of the **switch** anyway.

```
# include <stdio.h>
int main( )
{
    int  i = 2 ;
```

```
    switch ( i )
    {
        case 1 :
            printf ( "I am in case 1 \n" ) ;
            break ;
        case 2 :
            printf ( "I am in case 2 \n" ) ;
            break ;
        case 3 :
            printf ( "I am in case 3 \n" ) ;
            break ;
        default :
            printf ( "I am in default \n" ) ;
    }
    return 0 ;
}
```

The output of this program would be:

I am in case 2

The operation of **switch** is shown in Figure 3.4 in the form of a flowchart for a better understanding.

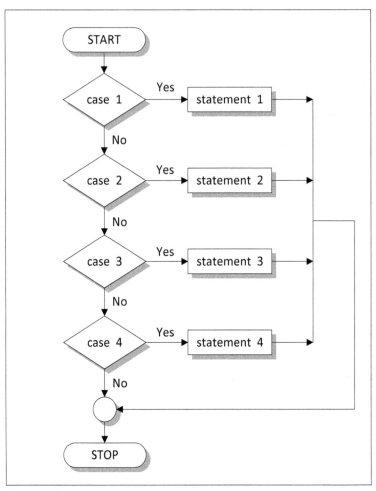

Figure 3.4

Tips and Traps

A few useful tips about the usage of **switch** and a few pitfalls to be avoided:

(a) The earlier program that used **switch** may give you the wrong impression that you can use only cases arranged in ascending order, 1, 2, 3 and default. You can, in fact, put the cases in any order you please.

(b) You are also allowed to use **char** values in **case** and **switch**

(c) At times we may want to execute a common set of statements for multiple **case**s. The following example shows how this can be achieved:

```
# include <stdio.h>
int main( )
{
    char ch ;

    printf ( "Enter any one of the alphabets a, b, or c " ) ;
    scanf ( "%c", &ch ) ;

    switch ( ch )
    {
        case 'a' :
        case 'A' :
            printf ( "a as in ashar\n" ) ;
            break ;
        case 'b' :
        case 'B' :
            printf ( "b as in brain\n" ) ;
            break ;

        return 0 ;
    }
}
```

Here, we are making use of the fact that once a **case** is satisfied; the control simply falls through the **switch** till it doesn't encounter a **break** statement. That is why if an alphabet **a** is entered, the **case** **'a'** is satisfied and since there are no statements to be executed in this **case**, the control automatically reaches the next **case**, i.e., **case** **'A'** and executes all the statements in this **case**.

(d) Even if there are multiple statements to be executed in each **case**, there is no need to enclose them within a pair of braces (unlike **if** and **else**).

(e) Every statement in a **switch** must belong to some **case** or the other. If a statement doesn't belong to any **case**, the compiler won't report an error. However, the statement would never get executed.

(f) If we have no **default** case, then the program simply falls through the entire **switch** and continues with the next instruction (if any,) that follows the closing brace of **switch**.

(g) The **break** statement when used in a **switch** takes the control outside the **switch**. However, use of **continue** will not take the control to the beginning of **switch** as one is likely to believe. This is because **switch** is not a looping statement unlike **while**, **for** or **do-while**.

(h) In principle, a **switch** may occur within another, but in practice, this is rarely done. Such statements would be called nested **switch** statements.

Loops

The versatility of the computer lies in its ability to perform a set of instructions repeatedly. This involves repeating some portion of the program either a specified number of times or until a particular condition is being satisfied. This repetitive operation is done through a loop control instruction.

There are three methods by way of which we can repeat a part of a program. They are:

(a) Using a **for** statement
(b) Using a **while** statement
(c) Using a **do-while** statement

Each of these methods is discussed in the following pages.

The *while* Loop

It is often the case in programming that you want to repeat something a fixed number of times. Perhaps you want to calculate gross salaries of ten different persons, or you want to convert temperatures from Centigrade to Fahrenheit for 15 different cities. The **while** loop is ideally suited for this.

Let us look at a simple example that uses a **while** loop to calculate simple interest for 3 sets of values of principal, number of years and rate of interest. The flowchart shown in Figure 3.5 would help you to understand the operation of the **while** loop.

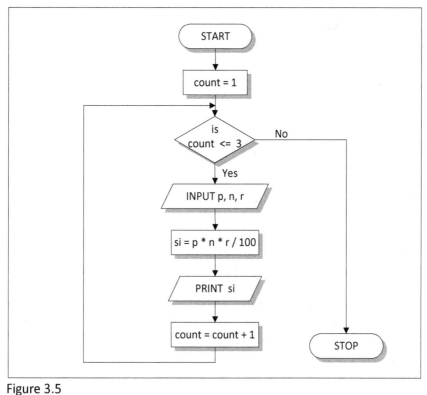

Figure 3.5

Let us now write a program that implements the logic of this flowchart.

```
/* Calculation of simple interest for 3 sets of p, n and r */
# include <stdio.h>
int main( )
{
    int   p, n, count ;
    float   r, si ;

    count = 1 ;
    while ( count <= 3 )
    {
        printf ( "\nEnter values of p, n and r " ) ;
        scanf ( "%d %d %f", &p, &n, &r ) ;
        si = p * n * r / 100 ;
        printf ( "Simple interest = Rs. %\nf", si ) ;

        count = count + 1 ;
```

```
    }
    return 0 ;
}
```

And here are a few sample runs of the program...

```
Enter values of p, n and r  1000  5  13.5
Simple interest = Rs. 675.000000
Enter values of p, n and r  2000  5  13.5
Simple interest = Rs. 1350.000000
Enter values of p, n and r  3500  5  3.5
Simple interest = Rs. 612.500000
```

The program executes all statements after the **while** 3 times. The logic for calculating the simple interest is written in these statements and they are enclosed within a pair of braces. These statements form the 'body' of the **while** loop. The parentheses after the **while** contain a condition. So long as this condition remains true the statements in the body of the **while** loop keep getting executed repeatedly. To begin with, the variable **count** is initialized to 1 and every time the simple interest logic is executed, the value of **count** is incremented by one. The variable **count** is often called either a 'loop counter' or an 'index variable'.

Tips and Traps

The general form of **while** is as shown below.

```
initialize loop counter ;
while ( test loop counter using a condition )
{
    do this ;
    and this ;
    increment loop counter ;
}
```

Note the following points about **while**...

– The statements within the **while** loop would keep getting executed till the condition being tested remains true. When the condition becomes false, the control passes to the first statement that follows the body of the **while** loop.

− In place of the condition there can be any other valid expression. So long as the expression evaluates to a non-zero value the statements within the loop would get executed.

− The condition being tested may use relational or logical operators as shown in the following examples:

```
while ( i <= 10 )
while ( i >= 10 && j <= 15 )
while ( j > 10 && ( b < 15 || c < 20 ) )
```

− The statements within the loop may be a single line or a block of statements. In the first case, the braces are optional. For example,

```
while ( i <= 10 )
   i = i + 1 ;
```

is same as

```
while ( i <= 10 )
{
   i = i + 1 ;
}
```

− Almost always, the while must test a condition that will eventually become false, otherwise the loop would be executed forever, indefinitely.

```
# include <stdio.h>
int main( )
{
   int  i = 1 ;
   while ( i <= 10 )
       printf ( "%d\n", i ) ;
   return 0 ;
}
```

This is an indefinite loop, since **i** remains equal to 1 forever. The correct form would be as under:

```
# include <stdio.h>
int main( )
{
```

```
    int  i = 1 ;
    while ( i <= 10 )
    {
        printf ( "%d\n", i ) ;
        i = i + 1 ;
    }
    return 0 ;
}
```

- Instead of incrementing a loop counter, we can decrement it and still manage to get the body of the loop executed repeatedly. This is shown below.

```
# include <stdio.h>
int main( )
{
    int  i = 5 ;
    while ( i >= 1 )
    {
        printf ( "Make the computer literate!\n" ) ;
        i = i - 1 ;
    }
}
```

- It is not necessary that a loop counter must only be an **int**. It can even be a **float**.

```
# include <stdio.h>
int main( )
{
    float  a = 10.0 ;
    while ( a <= 10.5 )
    {
        printf ( "Raindrops on roses..." ) ;
        printf ( "...and whiskers on kittens\n" ) ;
        a = a + 0.1 ;
    }
    return 0 ;
}
```

- Even floating point loop counters can be decremented. Once again, the increment and decrement could be by any value, not necessarily 1.

The *for* Loop

Perhaps one reason why few programmers use **while** is that they are too busy using the **for**, which is probably the most popular looping instruction. The **for** allows us to specify three things about a loop in a single line:

(a) Setting a loop counter to an initial value.

(b) Testing the loop counter to determine whether its value has reached the number of repetitions desired.

(c) Increasing the value of loop counter each time the body of the loop has been executed.

The general form of **for** statement is as under:

```
for ( initialize  counter ; test  counter ; increment  counter )
{
    do this ;
    and this ;
    and this ;
}
```

Let us now write down the simple interest program using **for**. Compare this program with the one that we wrote using **while**. The flowchart is also given in Figure 3.6 for a better understanding.

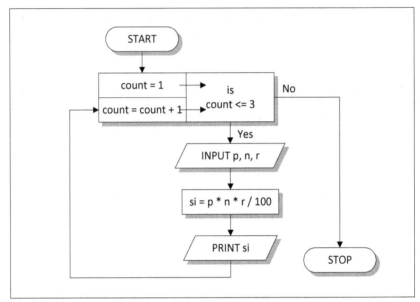

Figure 3.6

```
/* Calculation of simple interest for 3 sets of p, n and r */
# include <stdio.h>
int main( )
{
    int   p, n, count ;
    float   r, si ;

    for ( count = 1 ; count <= 3 ; count = count + 1 )
    {
        printf ( "Enter values of p, n, and r " ) ;
        scanf ( "%d %d %f", &p, &n, &r ) ;

        si = p * n * r / 100 ;
        printf ( "Simple Interest = Rs.%f\n", si ) ;
    }
    return 0 ;
}
```

If you compare this program with the one written using **while**, you can observe that the three steps—initialization, testing and incrementation—required for the loop construct have now been incorporated in the **for** statement.

Let us now examine how the **for** statement gets executed:

- When the **for** statement is executed for the first time, the value of **count** is set to an initial value 1.

- Next the condition **count <= 3** is tested. Since **count** is 1, the condition is satisfied and the body of the loop is executed for the first time.

- Upon reaching the closing brace of **for**, control is sent back to the **for** statement, where the value of **count** gets incremented by 1.

- Again the test is performed to check whether the new value of **count** exceeds 3.

- If the value of **count** is less than or equal to 3, the statements within the braces of **for** are executed again.

- The body of the **for** loop continues to get executed till **count** doesn't exceed the final value 3.

- When **count** reaches the value 4, the control exits from the loop and is transferred to the statement (if any) immediately after the body of **for**.

It is important to note that the initialization, testing and incrementation part of a **for** loop can be replaced by any valid expression. Thus the following **for** loops are perfectly ok.

```
for ( i = 10 ; i ; i -- )
    printf ( "%d ", i ) ;
for ( i < 4 ; j = 5 ; j = 0 )
    printf ( "%d ", i ) ;
for ( i = 1; i <=10 ; printf ( "%d ", i++ ) )
    ;
for ( scanf ( "%d", &i ) ; i <= 10 ; i++ )
    printf ( "%d", i ) ;
```

Multiple Initializations in the *for* Loop

The initialization expression in the **for** loop can contain more than one statement separated by a comma. For example,

```
for ( i = 1, j = 2 ; j <= 10 ; j++ )
```

Multiple statements can also be used in the incrementation expression of **for** loop; i.e., you can increment (or decrement) two or more variables at the same time. Similarly multiple conditions are allowed in the test expression. These conditions must be linked together using logical operators && and/or ||.

The *break* Statement

We often come across situations where we want to jump out of a loop instantly, without waiting to get back to the condition. The keyword **break** allows us to do this. When **break** is encountered inside any loop, control automatically passes to the first statement after the loop. A **break** is usually associated with an **if**. Let's consider the following example:

Example 3.5: Write a program to determine whether a number is prime or not. A prime number is said to be prime if it is divisible only by 1 or itself.

All we have to do to test whether a number is prime or not, is to divide it successively by all numbers from 2 to one less than itself. If remainder of any of these divisions is zero, the number is not a prime. If no division yields a zero then the number is a prime number. Following program implements this logic:

```c
# include <stdio.h>
int main( )
{
    int  num, i ;

    printf ( "Enter a number " ) ;
    scanf ( "%d", &num ) ;

    i = 2 ;
    while ( i <= num - 1 )
    {
        if ( num % i == 0 )
        {
            printf ( "Not a prime number\n" ) ;
            break ;
        }
        i++ ;
    }

    if ( i == num )
```

```
        printf ( "Prime number\n" ) ;
}
```

In this program, the moment **num % i** turns out to be zero, (i.e., **num** is exactly divisible by **i**), the message "Not a prime number" is printed and the control breaks out of the **while** loop. Why does the program require the **if** statement after the **while** loop at all? Well, there are two possibilities the control could have reached outside the **while** loop:

(a) It jumped out because the number proved to be not a prime.

(b) The loop came to an end because the value of **i** became equal to **num**.

When the loop terminates in the second case, it means that there was no number between 2 to **num - 1** that could exactly divide **num**. That is, **num** is indeed a prime. If this is true, the program should print out the message "Prime number".

The keyword **break**, breaks the control only from the **while** in which it is placed. Consider the following program, which illustrates this fact:

```
# include <stdio.h>
int main( )
{
    int i = 1 , j = 1 ;

    while ( i++ <= 100 )
    {
        while ( j++ <= 200 )
        {
            if ( j == 150 )
                break ;
            else
                printf ( "%d %d\n", i, j ) ;
        }
    }
    return 0 ;
}
```

In this program when **j** equals 150, **break** takes the control outside the inner **while** only, since it is placed inside the inner **while**.

The *continue* Statement

In some programming situations, we want to take the control to the beginning of the loop, bypassing the statements inside the loop, which have not yet been executed. The keyword **continue** allows us to do this. When **continue** is encountered inside any loop, control automatically passes to the beginning of the loop.

A **continue** is usually associated with an **if**. As an example, let's consider the following program:

```
# include <stdio.h>
int main( )
{
    int  i, j ;

    for ( i = 1 ; i <= 2 ; i++ )
    {
        for ( j = 1 ; j <= 2 ; j++ )
        {
            if ( i == j )
                continue ;

            printf ( "%d %d\n", i, j ) ;
        }
    }
    return 0 ;
}
```

The output of the above program would be...

```
1 2
2 1
```

Note that when the value of **i** equals that of **j**, the **continue** statement takes the control to the **for** loop (inner) bypassing the rest of the statements pending execution in the **for** loop (inner).

The *do-while* Loop

The **do-while** loop looks like this:

```
do
{
```

```
        this ;
        and this ;
        and this ;
        and this ;
} while ( this condition is true ) ;
```

There is a minor difference between the working of **while** and **do-while** loops. This difference is the place where the condition is tested. The **while** tests the condition before executing any of the statements within the **while** loop. As against this, the **do-while** tests the condition after having executed the statements within the loop.

What is a Function?

A function is a self-contained block of statements that perform a coherent task of some kind. Every C program can be thought of as a collection of these functions. As we noted earlier, using a function is something like hiring a person to do a specific job for you. Sometimes the interaction with this person is very simple; sometimes it's complex.

Suppose you have a task that is always performed exactly in the same way—say a bimonthly servicing of your motorbike. When you want it to be done, you go to the service station and say, "It's time, do it now". You don't need to give instructions, because the mechanic knows his job. You don't need to be told how the job is done. You assume the bike would be serviced in the usual way, the mechanic does it and that's that.

Let us now look at a simple C function that operates in much the same way as the mechanic. Actually, we will be looking at two things—a function that calls or activates the function and the function itself.

```c
# include <stdio.h>
void message( ) ; /* function prototype declaration */
int main( )
{
    message( ) ; /* function call */
    printf ( "Cry, and you stop the monotony!\n" ) ;
    return 0 ;
}
void message( ) /* function definition */
{
    printf ( "Smile, and the world smiles with you...\n" ) ;
}
```

And here's the output...

Smile, and the world smiles with you...
Cry, and you stop the monotony!

Here, we have defined two functions—**main( )** and **message( )**. In fact, we have used the word **message** at three places in the program. Let us understand the meaning of each.

The first is the function prototype declaration and is written as:

void message( ) ;

This prototype declaration indicates that **message( )** is a function which after completing its execution does not return any value. This 'does not return any value' is indicated using the keyword **void**. It is necessary to mention the prototype of every function that we intend to define in the program.

The second usage of **message** is...

```
void message( )
{
    printf ( "Smile, and the world smiles with you...\n" ) ;
}
```

This is the function definition. In this definition right now we are having only **printf( )**, but we can also use **if, for, while, switch**, etc., within this function definition.

The third usage is...

message( ) ;

Here the function **message( )** is being called by **main( )**. What do we mean when we say that **main( )** 'calls' the function **message( )**? We mean that the control passes to the function **message( )**. The activity of **main( )** is temporarily suspended; it falls asleep while the **message( )** function wakes up and goes to work. When the **message( )** function runs out of statements to execute, the control returns to **main( )**, which comes to life again and begins executing its code at the exact point where it left off. Thus, **main( )** becomes the 'calling' function, whereas **message( )** becomes the 'called' function.

If you have grasped the concept of 'calling' a function you are prepared for a call to more than one function. Consider the following example:

```c
# include <stdio.h>
void italy( ) ;
void brazil( ) ;
void argentina( ) ;
int main( )
{
    printf ( "I am in main\n" ) ;
    italy( ) ;
    brazil( ) ;
    argentina( ) ;
    return 0 ;
}
void italy( )
{
    printf ( "I am in italy\n" ) ;
}
void brazil( )
{
    printf ( "I am in brazil\n" ) ;
}
void argentina( )
{
    printf ( "I am in argentina\n" ) ;
}
```

The output of the above program when executed would be as under:

I am in main
I am in italy
I am in brazil
I am in argentina

A number of conclusions can be drawn from this program:

- A C program is a collection of one or more functions.

- If a C program contains only one function, it must be **main( )**.

- If a C program contains more than one function, then one (and only one) of these functions must be **main( )**, because program execution always begins with **main( )**.

- There is no limit on the number of functions that might be present in a C program.

- Each function in a program is called in the sequence specified by the function calls in **main( )**.

- After each function has done its thing, control returns to **main( )**. When **main( )** runs out of statements and function calls, the program ends.

As we have noted earlier, the program execution always begins with **main( )**. Except for this fact, all C functions enjoy a state of perfect equality. No precedence, no priorities, nobody is nobody's boss. Any function can call another function.

Let us now summarize what we have learnt so far.

(a) A function gets called when the function name is followed by a semicolon (;).

(b) A function is defined when function name is followed by a pair of braces ({ }) in which one or more statements may be present.

(c) Any function can be called from any other function. Even **main( )** can be called from other functions.

(d) A function can be called any number of times.

(e) The order in which the functions are defined in a program and the order in which they get called need not necessarily be same.

(f) A function can call itself. Such a process is called 'recursion'. We would discuss this aspect of C functions later in this Unit.

(g) A function can be called from another function, but a function cannot be defined in another function.

(h) There are basically two types of functions:

Library functions Ex. **printf( )**, **scanf( )**, etc.
User-defined functions Ex. **argentina( )**, **brazil( )**, etc.

As the name suggests, library functions are nothing but commonly required functions grouped together and stored in a Library file on the disk. These library of functions come ready-made with development environments like Turbo C, Visual Studio, NetBeans, gcc, etc. The procedure for calling both types of functions is exactly same.

Passing Values between Functions

The functions that we have used so far haven't been very flexible. We call them and they do what they are designed to do. It would be nice to have a little more control over what functions do. In short, now we want to communicate between the 'calling' and the 'called' functions.

The mechanism used to convey information to the function is the 'argument'. You have unknowingly used the arguments in the **printf( )** and **scanf( )** functions; the format string and the list of variables used inside the parentheses in these functions are arguments. The arguments are sometimes also called 'parameters'.

Consider the following program. In this program, in **main( )** we receive the values of **a**, **b** and **c** through the keyboard and then output the sum of **a**, **b** and **c**. However, the calculation of sum is done in a different function called **calsum( )**. If sum is to be calculated in **calsum( )** and values of **a**, **b** and **c** are received in **main( )**, then we must pass on these values to **calsum( )**, and once **calsum( )** calculates the sum, we must return it from **calsum( )** back to **main( )**.

```c
/* Sending and receiving values between functions */
# include <stdio.h>
int calsum ( int x, int y, int z ) ;
int main( )
{
    int a, b, c, sum ;
    printf ( "Enter any three numbers " ) ;
    scanf ( "%d %d %d", &a, &b, &c ) ;
    sum = calsum ( a, b, c ) ;
    printf ( "Sum = %d\n", sum ) ;
    return 0 ;
}
int calsum ( int x, int y, int z )
{
    int d ;

    d = x + y + z ;
    return ( d ) ;
}
```

And here is the output...

Enter any three numbers 10 20 30
Sum = 60

There are a number of things to note about this program:

(a) In this program, from the function **main( )**, the values of **a**, **b** and **c** are passed on to the function **calsum( )**, by making a call to the function **calsum( )** and mentioning **a**, **b** and **c** in the parentheses:

sum = calsum (a, b, c) ;

In the **calsum( )** function these values get collected in three variables **x**, **y** and **z**:

int calsum (int x, int y, int z)

(b) The variables **a**, **b** and **c** are called 'actual arguments', whereas the variables **x**, **y** and **z** are called 'formal arguments'. Any number of arguments can be passed to a function being called. However, the type, order and number of the actual and formal arguments must always be same.

In stead of using different variable names **x**, **y** and **z**, we could have used the same variable names **a**, **b** and **c**. But the compiler would still treat them as different variables since they are in different functions.

(c) Note the function prototype declaration of **calsum( )**. Instead of the usual **void**, we are using **int**. This indicates that **calsum( )** is going to return a value of the type **int**. It is not compulsory to use variable names in the prototype declaration. Hence we could as well have written the prototype as:

int calsum (int, int, int) ;

In the definition of **calsum** too, **void** has been replaced by **int**.

(d) In the earlier programs, the moment closing brace (**}**) of the called function was encountered, the control returned to the calling function. No separate **return** statement was necessary to send back the control.

This approach is fine if the called function is not going to return any meaningful value to the calling function. In the above program, however, we want to return the sum of **x**, **y** and **z**. Therefore, it is necessary to use the **return** statement.

The **return** statement serves two purposes:

(1) On executing the **return** statement, it immediately transfers the control back to the calling function.

(2) It returns the value present in the parentheses after **return**, to the calling function. In the above program, the value of sum of three numbers is being returned.

(e) There is no restriction on the number of **return** statements that may be present in a function. Also, the **return** statement need not always be present at the end of the called function. The following program illustrates these facts:

```
int fun( )
{
    int n ;
    printf ( "Enter any number " ) ;
    scanf ( "%d", &n ) ;
    if ( n >= 10 && n <= 90 )
        return ( n ) ;
    else
        return ( n + 32 ) ;
}
```

In this function, different **return** statements will be executed depending on whether **n** is between 10 and 90 or not.

(f) Whenever the control returns from a function, the sum being returned is collected in the calling function by assigning the called function to some variable. For example,

```
sum = calsum ( a, b, c ) ;
```

(g) All the following are valid **return** statements.

```
return ( a ) ;
return ( 23 ) ;
return ;
```

In the last statement, a garbage value is returned to the calling function since we are not returning any specific value. Note that, in this case, the parentheses after **return** are dropped. In the other **return** statements too, the parentheses can be dropped.

(h) A function can return only one value at a time. Thus, the following statements are invalid:

```
return ( a, b ) ;
return ( x, 12 ) ;
```

(i) If the value of a formal argument is changed in the called function, the corresponding change does not take place in the calling function. For example,

```
# include <stdio.h>
void fun ( int ) ;
int main( )
{
    int  a = 30 ;
    fun ( a ) ;
    printf ( "%d\n", a ) ;
    return 0 ;
}
void fun ( int  b )
{
    b = 60 ;
    printf ( "%d\n", b ) ;
}
```

The output of the above program would be:

```
60
30
```

Thus, even though the value of **b** is changed in **fun( )**, the value of **a** in **main( )** remains unchanged. This means that when values are passed to a called function, the values present in actual arguments are not physically moved to the formal arguments; just a photocopy of values in actual argument is made into formal arguments.

Return Type of Function

Suppose we want to find out square of a floating point number using a function. This is how this simple program would look like:

```
# include <stdio.h>
float square ( float ) ;
int main( )
{
    float  a, b ;
    printf ( "Enter any number " ) ;
    scanf ( "%f", &a ) ;
    b = square ( a ) ;
    printf ( "Square of %f is %f\n", a, b ) ;
    return 0 ;
}
float square ( float  x )
{
    float  y ;
    y = x * x ;
    return ( y ) ;
}
```

And here are three sample runs of this program...

```
Enter any number 3
Square of 3 is 9.000000
Enter any number 1.5
Square of 1.5 is 2.250000
Enter any number 2.5
Square of 2.5 is 6.250000
```

Since we are returning a **float** value from this function we have indicated the return type of the **square( )** function as **float** in the prototype declaration as well as in the function definition. Had we dropped **float** from the prototype and the definition, the compiler would have assumed that **square( )** is supposed to return an integer value.

Recursion

In C, it is possible for the functions to call themselves. A function is called 'recursive' if a statement within the body of a function calls the same function. Sometimes called 'circular definition', recursion is thus the process of defining something in terms of itself.

Let us now see a simple example of recursion. Suppose we want to calculate the factorial value of an integer. As we know, the factorial of a number is the product of all the integers between 1 and that number.

For example, 4 factorial is 4 * 3 * 2 * 1. This can also be expressed as 4! = 4 * 3! where '!' stands for factorial. Thus factorial of a number can be expressed in the form of itself. Hence this can be programmed using recursion. However, before we try to write a recursive function for calculating factorial let us take a look at the non-recursive function for calculating the factorial value of an integer.

```c
# include <stdio.h>
int factorial ( int ) ;
int main( )
{
    int  a, fact ;

    printf ( "Enter any number " ) ;
    scanf ( "%d", &a ) ;

    fact = factorial ( a ) ;
    printf ( "Factorial value = %d\n", fact ) ;
    return 0 ;
}

int factorial ( int  x )
{
    int  f = 1, i ;

    for ( i = x ; i >= 1 ; i-- )
        f = f * i ;

    return ( f ) ;
}
```

And here is the output...

Enter any number 3
Factorial value = 6

Work through the above program carefully, till you understand the logic of the program properly. Recursive factorial function can be understood only if you are thorough with the above logic.

Following is the recursive version of the function to calculate the factorial value:

```
# include <stdio.h>
int rec ( int ) ;
int main( )
{
    int  a, fact ;

    printf ( "Enter any number " ) ;
    scanf ( "%d", &a ) ;

    fact = rec ( a ) ;
    printf ( "Factorial value = %d\n", fact ) ;
    return 0 ;
}

int  rec ( int  x )
{
    int  f ;

    if ( x == 1 )
        return ( 1 ) ;
    else
        f = x * rec ( x - 1 ) ;

    return ( f ) ;
}
```

And here is the output for four runs of the program...

Enter any number 1
Factorial value = 1
Enter any number 2
Factorial value = 2
Enter any number 3
Factorial value = 6
Enter any number 5
Factorial value = 120

Let us understand this recursive factorial function thoroughly. In the first run when the number entered through **scanf( )** is 1, let us see what action does **rec( )** take. The value of **a** (i.e., 1) is copied into **x**. Since **x** turns out to be 1, the condition **if (x == 1)** is satisfied and hence 1 (which indeed is the value of 1 factorial) is returned through the **return** statement.

When the number entered through **scanf( )** is 2, the **(x == 1)** test fails, so we reach the statement,

f = x * rec (x - 1) ;

And here is where we meet recursion. How do we handle the expression **x * rec (x - 1)**? We multiply **x** by **rec (x - 1)**. Since the current value of **x** is 2, it is same as saying that we must calculate the value (2 * rec (1)). We know that the value returned by **rec (1)** is 1, so the expression reduces to (2 * 1), or simply 2. Thus the statement,

x * rec (x - 1) ;

evaluates to 2, which is stored in the variable **f**, and is returned to **main( )**, where it is duly printed as

Factorial value = 2

Now perhaps you can see what would happen if the value of **a** is 3, 4, 5 and so on.

In case the value of **a** is 5, **main( )** would call **rec( )** with 5 as its actual argument, and **rec( )** will send back the computed value. But before sending the computed value, **rec( )** calls **rec( )** and waits for a value to be returned. It is possible for the **rec( )** that has just been called to call yet another **rec( )**, the argument **x** being decreased in value by 1 for each of these recursive calls. We speak of this series of calls to **rec( )** as being different invocations of **rec( )**. These successive invocations of the same function are possible because the C compiler keeps track of which invocation calls which. These recursive invocations end finally when the last invocation gets an argument value of 1, which the preceding invocation of **rec( )** now uses to calculate its own **f** value and so on up the ladder. So we might say what happens is,

rec (5) returns (5 times rec (4),
    which returns (4 times rec (3),
        which returns (3 times rec (2),
            which returns (2 times rec (1),
                which returns (1)))))

Foxed? Well, that is recursion for you in its simplest garbs. I hope you agree that it's difficult to visualize how the control flows from one function call to another. Possibly Figure 3.7 would make things a bit clearer.

Assume that the number entered through **scanf( )** is 3. Using Figure 3.7 let's visualize what exactly happens when the recursive function **rec( )** gets called. Go through the figure carefully. The first time when **rec( )** is called from **main( )**, **x** collects 3. From here, since **x** is not equal to 1, the **if** block is skipped and **rec( )** is called again with the argument (**x** – 1), i.e. 2. This is a recursive call. Since **x** is still not equal to 1, **rec( )** is called yet another time, with argument (2 - 1). This time as **x** is 1, control goes back to previous **rec( )** with the value 1, and **f** is evaluated as 2.

Similarly, each **rec( )** evaluates its **f** from the returned value, and finally 6 is returned to **main( )**. The sequence would be grasped better by following the arrows shown in Figure 3.7. Let it be clear that while executing the program, there do not exist so many copies of the function **rec( )**. These have been shown in the figure just to help you keep track of how the control flows during successive recursive calls.

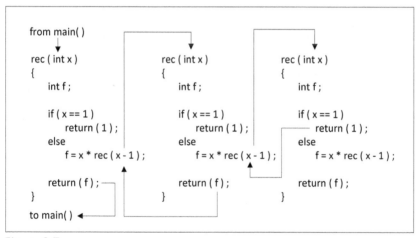

Figure 3.7

Recursion may seem strange and complicated at first glance, but it is often the most direct way to code an algorithm, and once you are familiar with recursion, the clearest way of doing so.

Exercise

[A] What will be the output of the following programs:

(a)
```c
# include <stdio.h>
int main( )
{
    int  a = 300, b, c ;
    if ( a >= 400 )
        b = 300 ;
    c = 200 ;
    printf ( "%d %d\n", b, c ) ;
    return 0 ;
}
```

(b)
```c
# include <stdio.h>
int main( )
{
    int  a = 500, b, c ;
    if ( a >= 400 )
        b = 300 ;
    c = 200 ;
    printf ( "%d %d\n", b, c ) ;
    return 0 ;
}
```

(c)
```c
# include <stdio.h>
int main( )
{
    int  x = 10, y = 20 ;
    if ( x == y ) ;
        printf ( "%d %d\n", x, y ) ;
    return 0 ;
}
```

(d)
```c
#include <stdio.h>
int main( )
{
    int  i = 4, j = -1, k = 0, w, x, y, z ;
    w = i || j || k ;
    x = i && j && k ;
    y = i || j && k ;
    z = i && j || k ;
```

```
        printf ( "w = %d x = %d y = %d z = %d\n", w, x, y, z ) ;
        return 0 ;
    }
```

(e) ```
     # include <stdio.h>
     int main( )
     {
         int x = 20, y = 40, z = 45 ;
         if (x > y && x > z)
             printf ("biggest = %d\n", x) ;
         else if (y > x && y > z)
             printf ("biggest = %d\n", y) ;
         else if (z > x && z > y)
             printf ("biggest = %d\n", z) ;
         return 0 ;
     }
     ```

(f)  ```
     # include <stdio.h>
     int main( )
     {
         while ( 'a' < 'b' )
             printf ( "malayalam is a palindrome\n" ) ;
         return 0 ;
     }
     ```

(g) ```
     # include <stdio.h>
     int main( )
     {
         int i ;
         while (i = 10)
         {
             printf ("%d\n", i) ;
             i = i + 1 ;
         }
         return 0 ;
     }
     ```

**[B]** Point out the errors, if any, in the following programs:

(a)  ```
     # include <stdio.h>
     int main( )
     {
         float  a = 12.25, b = 12.52 ;
     ```

```
        if ( a = b )
            printf ( "a and b are equal\n" ) ;
        return 0 ;
    }
```

(b)
```
    # include <stdio.h>
    int main( )
    {
        int  j = 10, k = 12 ;
        if ( k >= j )
        {
            {
                k = j ;
                j = k ;
            }
        }
        return 0 ;
    }
```

(c)
```
    # include <stdio.h>
    int main( )
    {
        if ( 'X' < 'x' )
            printf ( "ascii value of X is smaller than that of x\n" ) ;
    }
```

(d)
```
    # include <stdio.h>
    int main( )
    {
        int  suite = 1 ;
        switch ( suite ) ;
        {
            case 0 ;
                printf ( "Club\n" ) ;
            case 1 ;
                printf ( "Diamond\n" ) ;
        }
        return 0 ;
    }
```

(e)
```
    # include <stdio.h>
    int main( )
    {
```

```
        int temp ;
        scanf ( "%d", &temp ) ;
        switch ( temp )
        {
            case ( temp <= 20 ) :
                printf ( "Oooooooohhhh! Damn cool!\n" ) ;
            case ( temp > 20 && temp <= 30 ) :
                printf ( "Rain rain here again!\n" ) ;
            case ( temp > 30 && temp <= 40 ) :
                printf ( "Wish I am on Everest\n" ) ;
            default :
                printf ( "Good old nagpur weather\n" ) ;
        }
        return 0 ;
    }
```

(f)
```
    # include <stdio.h>
    int addmult ( int, int )
    int main( )
    {
        int  i = 3, j = 4, k, l ;
        k = addmult ( i, j ) ;
        l = addmult ( i, j ) ;
        printf ( "%d %d\n", k, l ) ;
        return 0 ;
    }
    int addmult ( int  ii, int  jj )
    {
        int  kk, ll ;
        kk = ii + jj ;
        ll = ii * jj ;
        return ( kk, ll ) ;
    }
```

(g)
```
    # include <stdio.h>
    void message( ) ;
    int main( )
    {
        int  a ;
        a = message( ) ;
        return 0 ;
    }
```

```
void message( )
{
    printf ( "Viruses are written in C\n" ) ;
    return ;
}
```

[C] Attempt the following:

(a) If cost price and selling price of an item are input through the keyboard, write a program to determine whether the seller has made profit or incurred loss. Also determine how much profit he made or loss he incurred.

(b) Any integer is input through the keyboard. Write a program to find out whether it is an odd number or even number.

(c) Any year is input through the keyboard. Write a program to determine whether the year is a leap year or not.

(Hint: Use the % (modulus) operator)

(d) If the three sides of a triangle are entered through the keyboard, write a program to check whether the triangle is valid or not. The triangle is valid if the sum of two sides is greater than the largest of the three sides.

(e) If the three sides of a triangle are entered through the keyboard, write a program to check whether the triangle is isosceles, equilateral, scalene or right angled triangle.

(f) Write a program to find the factorial value of any number entered through the keyboard.

(g) Two numbers are entered through the keyboard. Write a program to find the value of one number raised to the power of another.

(h) Write a program to add first seven terms of the following series

$$\frac{1}{1!} + \frac{2}{2!} + \frac{3}{3!} + \ldots\ldots$$

using a **for** loop:

(i) Write a program to generate all combinations of 1, 2 and 3 using **for** loop.

(j) Any year is entered through the keyboard. Write a function to determine whether the year is a leap year or not.

(k) A positive integer is entered through the keyboard. Write a function to obtain the prime factors of this number.

For example, prime factors of 24 are 2, 2, 2 and 3, whereas prime factors of 35 are 5 and 7.

(l)   A 5-digit positive integer is entered through the keyboard, write a recursive and a non-recursive function to calculate sum of digits of the 5-digit number.

(m) A positive integer is entered through the keyboard, write a program to obtain the prime factors of the number. Modify the function suitably to obtain the prime factors recursively.

(n)   Write a recursive function to obtain the first 25 numbers of a Fibonacci sequence. In a Fibonacci sequence the sum of two successive terms gives the third term. Following are the first few terms of the Fibonacci sequence:

(o)   1 1 2 3 5 8 13 21 34 55 89...

Unit 4

Arrays

- What are Arrays
    A Simple Program Using Array
- More on Arrays
    Array Initialization
    Array Elements in Memory
    Bounds Checking
    Passing Array Elements to a Function
- Two-Dimensional Arrays
    Initializing a Two-Dimensional Array
    Memory Map of a Two-Dimensional Array
- Structures
- Why use Structures?
    Declaring a Structure
    Accessing Structure Elements
    How Structure Elements are Stored?
- Additional Features of Structures
- Unions
    Union of Structures
- Utility of Unions
- Enumerated Data Type
    Uses of Enumerated Data Type
    Are Enums Necessary?
- Exercise

C language provides a capability that enables the user to design a set of similar data types, called array. This chapter describes how arrays can be created and manipulated in C.

What are Arrays?

For understanding the arrays properly, let us consider the following program:

```
# include <stdio.h>
int main( )
{
    int x ;
    x = 5 ;
    x = 10 ;
    printf ( "x = %d\n", x ) ;
    return 0 ;
}
```

No doubt, this program will print the value of **x** as 10. Why so? Because, when a value 10 is assigned to **x**, the earlier value of **x**, i.e., 5 is lost. Thus, ordinary variables (the ones which we have used so far) are capable of holding only one value at a time (as in this example). However, there are situations in which we would want to store more than one value at a time in a single variable.

For example, suppose we wish to arrange the percentage marks obtained by 100 students in ascending order. In such a case, we have two options to store these marks in memory:

(a) Construct 100 variables to store percentage marks obtained by 100 different students, i.e., each variable containing one student's marks.

(b) Construct one variable (called array or subscripted variable) capable of storing or holding all the hundred values.

Obviously, the second alternative is better. A simple reason for this is, it would be much easier to handle one variable than handling 100 different variables. Moreover, there are certain logics that cannot be dealt with, without the use of an array. Now a formal definition of an array—An array is a collective name given to a group of 'similar quantities'. These similar quantities could be percentage marks of 100 students, or salaries of 300 employees, or ages of 50 employees. What is important is that the quantities must be 'similar'. Each member in the group is referred to by its position in the group. For example, assume the following group of numbers, which represent percentage marks obtained by five students.

per = { 48, 88, 34, 23, 96 }

If we want to refer to the second number of the group, the usual notation used is per$_2$. Similarly, the fourth number of the group is referred as per$_4$. However, in C, the fourth number is referred as **per[3].** This is because, in C, the counting of elements begins with 0 and not with 1. Thus, in this example **per[3]** refers to 23 and **per[4]** refers to 96. In general, the notation would be **per[i]**, where, **i** can take a value 0, 1, 2, 3, or 4, depending on the position of the element being referred. Here **per** is the subscripted variable (array), whereas **i** is its subscript.

Thus, an array is a collection of similar elements. These similar elements could be all **int**s, or all **float**s, or all **char**s, etc. Usually, the array of characters is called a 'string', whereas an array of **int**s or **float**s is called simply an array. Remember that all elements of any given array must be of the same type, i.e., we cannot have an array of 10 numbers, of which 5 are **int**s and 5 are **float**s.

A Simple Program using Array

Let us try to write a program to find average marks obtained by a class of 30 students in a test.

```
# include <stdio.h>
int main( )
{
    int  avg, sum = 0 ;
    int  i ;
    int  marks[ 30 ] ; /* array declaration */

    for ( i = 0 ; i <= 29 ; i++ )
    {
        printf ( "Enter marks " ) ;
        scanf ( "%d", &marks[ i ] ) ; /* store data in array */
    }

    for ( i = 0 ; i <= 29 ; i++ )
        sum = sum + marks[ i ] ; /* read data from an array*/
```

```
    avg = sum / 30 ;
    printf ( "Average marks = %d\n", avg ) ;
    return 0 ;
}
```

There is a lot of new material in this program, so let us take it apart slowly.

Array Declaration

To begin with, like other variables, an array needs to be declared so that the compiler will know what kind of an array and how large an array we want. In our program, we have done this with the statement:

int marks[30] ;

Here, **int** specifies the type of the variable, just as it does with ordinary variables and the word **marks** specifies the name of the variable. The [**30]** however is new. The number 30 tells how many elements of the type **int** will be in our array. This number is often called the 'dimension' of the array. The bracket ([ ]) tells the compiler that we are dealing with an array.

Accessing Elements of an Array

Once an array is declared, let us see how individual elements in the array can be referred. This is done with subscript, the number in the brackets following the array name. This number specifies the element's position in the array. All the array elements are numbered, starting with 0. Thus, **marks[2]** is not the second element of the array, but the third. In our program, we are using the variable **i** as a subscript to refer to various elements of the array. This variable can take different values and hence can refer to the different elements in the array in turn. This ability to use variables to represent subscripts is what makes arrays so useful.

Entering Data into an Array

Here is the section of code that places data into an array:

```
for ( i = 0 ; i <= 29 ; i++ )
{
    printf ( "Enter marks " ) ;
    scanf ( "%d", &marks[ i ] ) ;
}
```

The **for** loop causes the process of asking for and receiving a student's marks from the user to be repeated 30 times. The first time through the loop, **i** has a value 0, so the **scanf( )** function will cause the value typed to be stored in the array element **marks[0]**, the first element of the array. This process will be repeated until **i** becomes 29. This is last time through the loop, which is a good thing, because there is no array element like **marks[30]**.

In **scanf( )** function, we have used the "address of" operator (**&**) on the element **marks[i]** of the array, just as we have used it earlier on other variables (**&rate**, for example). In so doing, we are passing the address of this particular array element to the **scanf( )** function, rather than its value; which is what **scanf( )** requires.

Reading Data from an Array

The balance of the program reads the data back out of the array and uses it to calculate the average. The **for** loop is much the same, but now the body of the loop causes each student's marks to be added to a running total stored in a variable called **sum**. When all the marks have been added up, the result is divided by 30, the number of students, to get the average.

```
for ( i = 0 ; i <= 29 ; i++ )
    sum = sum + marks[ i ] ;

avg = sum / 30 ;
printf ( "Average marks = %d\n", avg ) ;
```

To fix our ideas, let us revise whatever we have learnt about arrays:

(a) An array is a collection of similar elements.
(b) The first element in the array is numbered 0, so the last element is 1 less than the size of the array.
(c) An array is also known as a subscripted variable.
(d) Before using an array, its type and dimension must be declared.
(e) However big an array, its elements are always stored in contiguous memory locations. This is a very important point which we would discuss in more detail later on.

More on Arrays

Array is a very popular data type with C programmers. This is because of the convenience with which arrays lend themselves to programming.

The features which make arrays so convenient to program would be discussed below, along with the possible pitfalls in using them.

Array Initialization

So far we have used arrays that did not have any values in them to begin with. We managed to store values in them during program execution. Let us now see how to initialize an array while declaring it. Following are a few examples that demonstrate this:

```
int  num[ 6 ] = { 2, 4, 12, 5, 45, 5 } ;
int  n[ ] = { 2, 4, 12, 5, 45, 5 } ;
float  press[ ] = { 12.3, 34.2, -23.4, -11.3 } ;
```

Note the following points carefully:

(a) Till the array elements are not given any specific values, they are supposed to contain garbage values.

(b) If the array is initialised where it is declared, mentioning the dimension of the array is optional as in the 2nd and 3rd examples above.

Array Elements in Memory

Consider the following array declaration:

```
int  arr[ 8 ] ;
```

What happens in memory when we make this declaration? 32 bytes get immediately reserved in memory, 4 bytes each for the 8 integers (under TC/TC++ the array would occupy 16 bytes as each integer would occupy 2 bytes). And since the array is not being initialized, all eight values present in it would be garbage values. This so happens because the storage class of this array is assumed to be **auto**. If the storage class is declared to be **static**, then all the array elements would have a default initial value as zero. Whatever be the initial values, all the array elements would always be present in contiguous memory locations. This arrangement of array elements in memory is shown in Figure 4.1.

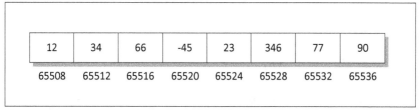

Figure 4.1

Bounds Checking

In C, there is no check to see if the subscript used for an array exceeds the size of the array. Data entered with a subscript exceeding the array size will simply be placed in memory outside the array; probably on top of other data, or on the program itself. This will lead to unpredictable results, to say the least, and there will be no error message to warn you that you are going beyond the array size. In some cases, the computer may just hang. Thus, the following program may turn out to be suicidal:

```
# include <stdio.h>
int main( )
{
    int  num[ 40 ], i ;

    for ( i = 0 ; i <= 100 ; i++ )
        num[ i ] = i ;
    return 0 ;
}
```

Thus, to see to it that we do not reach beyond the array size, is entirely the programmer's botheration and not the compiler's.

So far we have explored arrays with only one dimension. It is also possible for arrays to have two or more dimensions. Let us now see how multidimensional arrays can be created and manipulated in C.

Two-Dimensional Arrays

The two-dimensional array is also called a matrix. Let us see how to create this array and work with it. Here is a sample program that stores roll number and marks obtained by a student side-by-side in a matrix.

```
# include <stdio.h>
int main( )
{
```

```
int stud[ 4 ][ 2 ] ;
int i, j ;

for ( i = 0 ; i <= 3 ; i++ )
{
    printf ( "Enter roll no. and marks" ) ;
    scanf ( "%d %d", &stud[ i ][ 0 ], &stud[ i ][ 1 ] ) ;
}
for ( i = 0 ; i <= 3 ; i++ )
    printf ( "%d %d\n", stud[ i ][ 0 ], stud[ i ][ 1 ] ) ;

return 0 ;
}
```

There are two parts to the program—in the first part, through a **for** loop, we read in the values of roll no. and marks, whereas, in the second part through another **for** loop, we print out these values.

Look at the **scanf( )** statement used in the first **for** loop:

scanf ("%d %d", &stud[i][0], &stud[i][1]) ;

In **stud[i][0]** and **stud[i][1]**, the first subscript of the variable **stud**, is row number which changes for every student. The second subscript tells which of the two columns are we talking about—the zeroth column which contains the roll no. or the first column which contains the marks. Remember the counting of rows and columns begin with zero. The complete array arrangement is shown in Figure 4.2.

	column no. 0	column no. 1
row no. 0	1234	56
row no. 1	1212	33
row no. 2	1434	80
row no. 3	1312	78

Figure 4.2

Thus, 1234 is stored in **stud[0][0]**, 56 is stored in **stud[0][1]** and so on. The above arrangement highlights the fact that a two- dimensional array is nothing but a collection of a number of one- dimensional arrays placed one below the other.

In our sample program, the array elements have been stored row-wise and accessed row-wise. However, you can access the array elements column-wise as well. Traditionally, the array elements are being stored and accessed row-wise; therefore we would also stick to the same strategy.

Initializing a Two-Dimensional Array

How do we initialize a two-dimensional array? As simple as this...

```
int stud[ 4 ][ 2 ] = {
                     { 1234, 56 },
                     { 1212, 33 },
                     { 1434, 80 },
                     { 1312, 78 }
              } ;
```

or even this would work...

```
int stud[ 4 ][ 2 ] = { 1234, 56, 1212, 33, 1434, 80, 1312, 78 } ;
```

of course, with a corresponding loss in readability.

It is important to remember that, while initializing a 2-D array, it is necessary to mention the second (column) dimension, whereas the first dimension (row) is optional.

Thus the declarations,

```
int arr[ 2 ][ 3 ] = { 12, 34, 23, 45, 56, 45 } ;
int arr[  ][ 3 ] = { 12, 34, 23, 45, 56, 45 } ;
```

are perfectly acceptable,

whereas,

```
int arr[ 2 ][  ] = { 12, 34, 23, 45, 56, 45 } ;
int arr[  ][  ] = { 12, 34, 23, 45, 56, 45 } ;
```

would never work.

Memory Map of a Two-Dimensional Array

Let us reiterate the arrangement of array elements in a two-dimensional array of students, which contains roll nos. in one column and the marks in the other.

The array arrangement shown in Figure 4.2 is only conceptually true. This is because memory doesn't contain rows and columns. In memory, whether it is a one-dimensional or a two-dimensional array, the array elements are stored in one continuous chain. The arrangement of array elements of a two-dimensional array in memory is shown in Figure 4.3:

s[0][0]	s[0][1]	s[1][0]	s[1][1]	s[2][0]	s[2][1]	s[3][0]	s[3][1]
1234	56	1212	33	1434	80	1312	78
65508	65512	65516	65520	65524	65528	65532	65536

Figure 4.3

We can easily refer to the marks obtained by the third student using the subscript notation as shown below.

printf ("Marks of third student = %d", stud[2][1]) ;

Can we not refer to the same element using pointer notation, the way we did in one-dimensional arrays? Answer is yes. Only the procedure is slightly difficult to understand. So, read on...

Structures

Which mechanic is good enough who knows how to repair only one type of vehicle? None. Same thing is true about C language. It wouldn't have been so popular had it been able to handle only all **int**s, or all **float**s or all **char**s at a time. In fact, when we handle real world data, we don't usually deal with little atoms of information by themselves—things like integers, characters and such. Instead, we deal with entities that are collections of things, each thing having its own attributes, just as the entity we call a 'book' is a collection of things, such as title, author, call number, publisher, number of pages, date of publication, etc. As you can see, all this data is dissimilar, like author is a string, whereas number of pages is an integer. For dealing with such collections, C provides a data type called 'structure'. Thus a structure gathers together, different atoms of information that comprise a given entity.

Why use Structures?

We have seen earlier how ordinary variables can hold one piece of information and how arrays can hold a number of pieces of information of the same data type. These two data types can handle a great variety of situations. But quite often we deal with entities that are collection of dissimilar data types.

For example, suppose you want to store data about a book. You might want to store its name (a string), its price (a float) and number of pages in it (an int). If data about say 3 such books is to be stored, then we can follow two approaches:

(a) Construct individual arrays, one for storing names, another for storing prices and still another for storing number of pages.

(b) Use a structure variable.

Let us examine these two approaches one-by-one. For the sake of programming convenience, assume that the names of books would be single character long. Let us begin with a program that uses arrays.

```
# include <stdio.h>
int main( )
{
    char  name[ 3 ] ;
    float  price[ 3 ] ;
    int  pages[ 3 ], i ;

    printf ( "Enter names, prices and no. of pages of 3 books\n" ) ;

    for ( i = 0 ; i <= 2 ; i++ )
        scanf ( "%c %f %d", &name[ i ], &price[ i ], &pages[ i ] ) ;

    printf ( "\nAnd this is what you entered\n" ) ;
    for ( i = 0 ; i <= 2 ; i++ )
        printf ( "%c %f %d\n", name[ i ], price[ i ], pages[ i ] ) ;
    return 0 ;
}
```

And here is the sample run...

Enter names, prices and no. of pages of 3 books
A 100.00 354

C 256.50 682
F 233.70 512

And this is what you entered
A 100.000000 354
C 256.500000 682
F 233.700000 512

This approach, no doubt, allows you to store names, prices and number of pages. But as you must have realized, it is an unwieldy approach that obscures the fact that you are dealing with a group of characteristics related to a single entity—the book.

The program becomes more difficult to handle as the number of items relating to the book goes on increasing. For example, we would be required to use a number of arrays, if we also decide to store name of the publisher, date of purchase of book, etc. To solve this problem, C provides a special data type—the structure.

A structure contains a number of data types grouped together. These data types may or may not be of the same type. The following example illustrates the use of this data type:

```c
# include <stdio.h>
int main( )
{
    struct book
    {
        char  name ;
        float  price ;
        int  pages ;
    } ;
    struct book  b1, b2, b3 ;

    printf ( "Enter names, prices & no. of pages of 3 books\n" ) ;
    scanf ( "%c %f %d", &b1.name, &b1.price, &b1.pages ) ;
    scanf ( "%c %f %d", &b2.name, &b2.price, &b2.pages ) ;
    scanf ( "%c %f %d", &b3.name, &b3.price, &b3.pages ) ;
    printf ( "And this is what you entered\n" ) ;
    printf ( "%c %f %d\n", b1.name, b1.price, b1.pages ) ;
    printf ( "%c %f %d\n", b2.name, b2.price, b2.pages ) ;
    printf ( "%c %f %d\n", b3.name, b3.price, b3.pages ) ;
    return 0 ;
```

}

And here is the output...

Enter names, prices and no. of pages of 3 books
A 100.00 354
C 256.50 682
F 233.70 512
And this is what you entered
A 100.000000 354
C 256.500000 682
F 233.700000 512

This program demonstrates two fundamental aspects of structures:

(a)   Declaration of a structure
(b)   Accessing of structure elements

Let us now look at these concepts one-by-one.

Declaring a Structure

In our example program, the following statement declares the structure type:

```
struct book
{
    char  name ;
    float  price ;
    int  pages ;
} ;
```

This statement defines a new data type called **struct book**. Each variable of this data type will consist of a character variable called **name**, a float variable called **price** and an integer variable called **pages**. The general form of a structure declaration statement is given below.

```
struct <structure name>
{
    structure element 1 ;
    structure element 2 ;
    structure element 3 ;
    ......
    ......
```

```
};
```

Once the new structure data type has been defined, one or more variables can be declared to be of that type. For example, the variables **b1**, **b2**, **b3** can be declared to be of the type **struct book**, as,

```
struct book b1, b2, b3 ;
```

This statement sets aside space in memory. It makes available space to hold all the elements in the structure—in this case, 7 bytes—one for **name**, four for **price** and two for **pages**. These bytes are always in adjacent memory locations.

If we so desire, we can combine the declaration of the structure type and the structure variables in one statement.

For example,

```
struct book
{
    char name ;
    float price ;
    int pages ;
};
struct book b1, b2, b3 ;
```

is same as...

```
struct book
{
    char name ;
    float price ;
    int pages ;
} b1, b2, b3 ;
```

or even...

```
struct
{
    char name ;
    float price ;
    int pages ;
} b1, b2, b3 ;
```

Like primary variables and arrays, structure variables can also be initialized where they are declared. The format used is quite similar to that used to initialize arrays.

```
struct book
{
    char name[ 10 ] ;
    float price ;
    int pages ;
} ;
struct book b1 = { "Basic", 130.00, 550 } ;
struct book b2 = { "Physics", 150.80, 800 } ;
struct book b3 = { 0 } ;
```

Note the following points while declaring a structure type:

(a) The closing brace (}) in the structure type declaration must be followed by a semicolon (;).

(b) It is important to understand that a structure type declaration does not tell the compiler to reserve any space in memory. All a structure declaration does is, it defines the 'form' of the structure.

(c) Usually structure type declaration appears at the top of the source code file, before any variables or functions are defined. In very large programs they are usually put in a separate header file, and the file is included (using the preprocessor directive **#include**) in whichever program we want to use this structure type.

(d) If a structure variable is initiated to a value { 0 }, then all its elements are set to value 0, as in **b3** above. This is a handy way of initializing structure variables. In absence of this, we would have been required to initialize each individual element to a value 0.

Accessing Structure Elements

Having declared the structure type and the structure variables, let us see how the elements of the structure can be accessed.

In arrays, we can access individual elements of an array using a subscript. Structures use a different scheme. They use a dot (.) operator. So to refer to **pages** of the structure defined in our sample program, we have to use,

b1.pages

Similarly, to refer to **price**, we would use,

b1.price

Note that before the dot, there must always be a structure variable and after the dot, there must always be a structure element.

How Structure Elements are Stored?

Whatever be the elements of a structure, they are always stored in contiguous memory locations. The following program would illustrate this:

```
/* Memory map of structure elements */
# include <stdio.h>
int main( )
{
    struct book
    {
        char name ;
        float price ;
        int pages ;
    } ;
    struct book  b1 = { 'B', 130.00, 550 } ;

    printf ( "Address of name = %u\n", &b1.name ) ;
    printf ( "Address of price = %u\n", &b1.price ) ;
    printf ( "Address of pages = %u\n", &b1.pages ) ;
    return 0 ;
}
```

Here is the output of the program...

Address of name = 65518
Address of price = 65519
Address of pages = 65523

Actually, the structure elements are stored in memory as shown in the Figure 4.4.

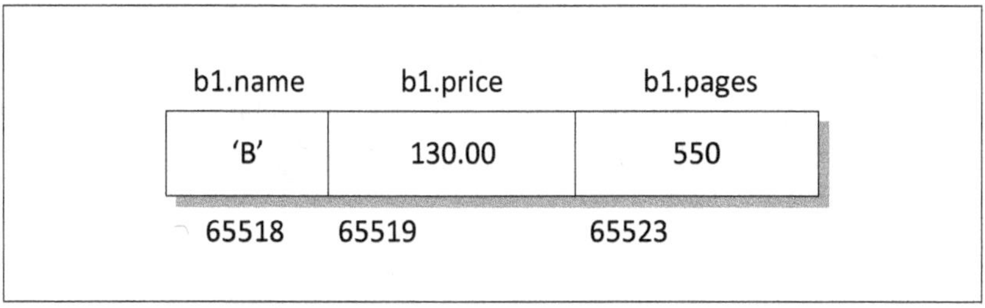

Figure 4.4

Additional Features of Structures

Let us now explore the intricacies of structures with a view of programming convenience. We would highlight these intricacies with suitable examples.

(a) The values of a structure variable can be assigned to another structure variable of the same type using the assignment operator. It is not necessary to copy the structure elements piece-meal. Obviously, programmers prefer assignment to piece-meal copying. This is shown in the following example:

```
# include <stdio.h>
# include <string.h>
int main( )
{
    struct employee
    {
        char  name[ 10 ] ;
        int  age ;
        float  salary ;
    } ;
    struct employee  e1 = { "Sanjay", 30, 5500.50 } ;
    struct employee  e2, e3 ;

    /* piece-meal copying */
    strcpy ( e2.name, e1.name ) ;
     /* e2.name = e1. name is wrong */
    e2.age = e1.age ;
    e2.salary = e1.salary ;

    /* copying all elements at one go */
    e3 = e2 ;
```

```
        printf ( "%s %d %f\n", e1.name, e1.age, e1.salary ) ;
        printf ( "%s %d %f\n", e2.name, e2.age, e2.salary ) ;
        printf ( "%s %d %f\n", e3.name, e3.age, e3.salary ) ;
        return 0 ;
}
```

The output of the program would be...

Sanjay 30 5500.500000
Sanjay 30 5500.500000
Sanjay 30 5500.500000

Ability to copy the contents of all structure elements of one variable into the corresponding elements of another structure variable is rather surprising, since C does not allow assigning the contents of one array to another just by equating the two. As we saw earlier, for copying arrays, we have to copy the contents of the array element-by-element.

This copying of all structure elements at one go has been possible only because the structure elements are stored in contiguous memory locations. Had this not been so, we would have been required to copy structure variables element by element. And who knows, had this been so, structures would not have become popular at all.

(b) One structure can be nested within another structure. Using this facility, complex data types can be created. The following program shows nested structures at work:

```
# include <stdio.h>
int main( )
{
    struct address
    {
        char  phone[ 15 ] ;
        char  city[ 25 ] ;
        int  pin ;
    } ;

    struct emp
    {
```

```
            char  name[ 25 ] ;
            struct address  a ;
    } ;
    struct emp  e = { "jeru", "531046", "nagpur", 10 };

    printf ( "name = %s phone = %s\n", e.name, e.a.phone ) ;
    printf ( "city = %s pin = %d\n", e.a.city, e.a.pin ) ;
    return 0 ;
}
```

And here is the output...

```
name = jeru phone = 531046
city = nagpur pin = 10
```

Notice the method used to access the element of a structure that is part of another structure. For this, the dot operator is used twice, as in the expression,

e.a.pin or e.a.city

Of course, the nesting process need not stop at this level. We can nest a structure within a structure, within another structure, which is in still another structure and so on... till the time we can comprehend the structure ourselves. Such construction, however, gives rise to variable names that can be surprisingly self-descriptive, for example:

maruti.engine.bolt.large.qty

This clearly signifies that we are referring to the quantity of large sized bolts that fit on an engine of a Maruti car.

Unions

Unions are derived data types, the way structures are. Unions and structures look alike, but are engaged in totally different activities.

Both structures and unions are used to group a number of different variables together. But while a structure enables us treat a number of different variables stored at different places in memory, a union enables us to treat the same space in memory as a number of different variables. That is, a union offers a way for a section of memory to be treated as a variable of one type on one occasion, and as a different variable of a different type on another occasion.

You might wonder why it would be necessary to do such a thing, but we will be seeing several very practical applications of unions soon. First, let us take a look at a simple example.

```c
/* Demo of union at work */
# include <stdio.h>
int main( )
{
    union a
    {
        short int i ;
        char ch[ 2 ] ;
    } ;
    union a key ;

    key.i = 512 ;
    printf ( "key.i = %d\n", key.i ) ;
    printf ( "key.ch[ 0 ] = %d\n", key.ch[ 0 ] ) ;
    printf ( "key.ch[ 1 ] = %d\n", key.ch[ 1 ] ) ;
    return 0 ;
}
```

And here is the output...

```
key.i = 512
key.ch[ 0 ] = 0
key.ch[ 1 ] = 2
```

As you can see, first we declared a data type of the type **union a**, and then a variable **key** to be of the type **union a**. This is similar to the way we first declare the structure type and then the structure variables. Also, the union elements are accessed exactly the same way in which the structure elements are accessed, using a '.' operator. However, the similarity ends here. To illustrate this let us compare the following data types:

```c
struct a
{
    short int i ;
    char ch[ 2 ] ;
```

```
};
struct a key ;
```

This data type would occupy 4 bytes in memory, 2 for **key.i** and 1 each for **key.ch[0]** and **key.ch[1]**, as shown in Figure 4.5.

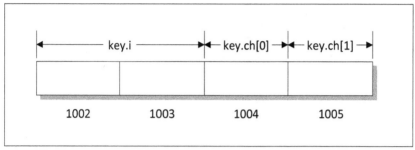

Figure 4.5

Now we declare a similar data type, but instead of using a structure we use a union.

```
union a
{
    short int i ;
    char ch[ 2 ] ;
};
union a key ;
```

Representation of this data type in memory is shown in Figure 4.6.

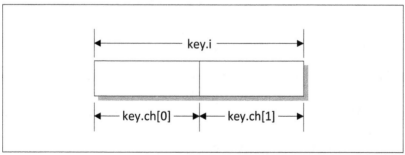

Figure 4.6

As shown in Figure 4.6, the union occupies only 2 bytes in memory. Note that the same memory locations that are used for **key.i** are also being used by **key.ch[0]** and **key.ch[1]**. It means that the memory locations used by **key.i** can also be accessed using **key.ch[0]** and **key.ch[1]**.

What purpose does this serve? Well, now we can access the 2 bytes simultaneously (by using **key.i**) or the same 2 bytes individually (using **key.ch[0]** and **key.ch[1]**).

This is a frequent requirement while interacting with the hardware, i.e., sometimes we are required to access 2 bytes simultaneously and sometimes each byte individually. Faced with such a situation, using union is the answer, usually.

Perhaps you would be able to understand the union data type more thoroughly if we take a fresh look at the output of the above program. Here it is...

key.i = 512
key.ch[0] = 0
key.ch[1] = 2

Let us understand this output in detail. 512 is an integer, a 2 byte number. Its binary equivalent will be 0000 0010 0000 0000. We would expect that this binary number when stored in memory would look as shown in Figure 4.7.

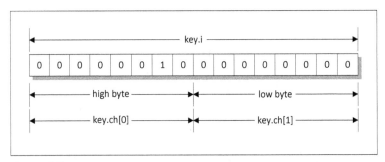

Figure 4.7

If the number is stored in this manner, then the output of **key.ch[0]** and **key.ch[1]** should have been 2 and 0, respectively. But, if you look at the output of the program written above, it is exactly the opposite. Why is it so? Because, in CPUs that follow little-endian architecture (Intel CPUs, for example), when a 2-byte number is stored in memory, the low byte is stored before the high byte. It means, actually 512 would be stored in memory as shown in Figure 4.8. In CPUs with big-endian architecture this reversal of bytes does not happen.

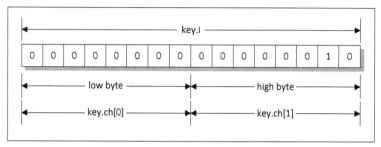

Figure 4.8

Now, we can see why value of **key.ch[0]** is printed as 0 and value of **key.ch[1]** is printed as 2.

One last thing. We can't assign different values to the different union elements at the same time. That is, if we assign a value to **key.i**, it gets automatically assigned to **key.ch[0]** and **key.ch[1]**. Vice versa, if we assign a value to **key.ch[0]** or **key.ch[1]**, it is bound to get assigned to **key.i**. Here is a program that illustrates this fact.

```
# include <stdio.h>
int main( )
{
    union a
    {
        short int i ;
        char ch[ 2 ] ;
    } ;
    union a key ;

    key.i = 512 ;
    printf ( "key.i = %d\n", key.i ) ;
    printf ( "key.ch[ 0 ] = %d\n", key.ch[ 0 ] ) ;
    printf ( "key.ch[ 1 ] = %d\n", key.ch[ 1 ] ) ;

    key.ch[ 0 ] = 50 ; /* assign a new value to key.ch[ 0 ] */
    printf ( "key.i = %d\n", key.i ) ;
    printf ( "key.ch[ 0 ] = %d\n", key.ch[ 0 ] ) ;
    printf ( "key.ch[ 1 ] = %d\n", key.ch[ 1 ] ) ;
    return 0 ;
}
```

And here is the output...

```
key.i = 512
key.ch[ 0 ] = 0
key.ch[ 1 ] = 2
key.i= 562
key.ch[ 0 ] = 50
key.ch[ 1 ] = 2
```

Before we move on to the next section, let us reiterate that a union provides a way to look at the same data in several different ways. For example, there can exist a union as shown below.

```
union  b
{
    double  d ;
    float  f[ 2 ] ;
    short  int  i[ 4 ] ;
    char  ch[ 8 ] ;
} ;
union  b  data ;
```

In what different ways can the data be accessed from it? Sometimes, as a complete set of 8 bytes (**data.d**), sometimes as two sets of 4 bytes each (**data.f[0]** and **data.f[1]**), sometimes as four sets of 2 bytes each (**data.i[0], data.i[1], data.i[2]** and **data.[3]**) and sometimes as 8 individual bytes (**data.ch[0], data.ch[1]... data.ch[7]**).

Also note that there can exist a union, each of whose elements is of different size. In such a case, the size of the union variable will be equal to the size of the longest element in the union.

Union of Structures

Just as one structure can be nested within another, a union too can be nested in another union. Not only that, there can be a union in a structure, or a structure in a union. Here is an example of structures nested in a union.

```
# include <stdio.h>
int main( )
{
    struct  a
    {
        int  i ;
```

```
        char c[ 2 ] ;
    } ;
    struct  b
    {
        int  j ;
        char  d[ 2 ] ;
    } ;
    union  z
    {
        struct  a  key ;
        struct  b  data ;
    } ;
    union  z  strange ;

    strange.key.i = 512 ;
    strange.data.d[ 0 ] = 0 ;
    strange.data.d[ 1 ] = 32 ;

    printf ( "%d\n", strange.key.i ) ;
    printf ( "%d\n", strange.data.j ) ;
    printf ( "%d\n", strange.key.c[ 0 ] ) ;
    printf ( "%d\n", strange.data.d[ 0 ] ) ;
    printf ( "%d\n", strange.key.c[ 1 ] ) ;
    printf ( "%d\n", strange.data.d[ 1 ] ) ;
    return 0 ;
}
```

And here is the output...

```
512
512
0
0
32
32
```

Just as we do with nested structures, we access the elements of the union in this program using the '.' operator twice. Thus,

strange.key.i

refers to the variable **i** in the structure **key** in the union **strange**. Analysis of the output of the above program is left to the reader.

Utility of Unions

Suppose we wish to store information about employees in an organization. The items of information are as shown below.

Name
Grade
Age
If Grade = HSK (Highly Skilled)
    hobbie name
    credit card no.
If Grade = SSK (Semi Skilled)
    Vehicle no.
    Distance from Co.

Since this is dissimilar information we can gather it together using a structure as shown below.

```
struct employee
{
    char  n[ 20 ] ;
    char  grade[ 4 ] ;
    int  age ;
    char  hobby[ 10 ] ;
    int  crcardno ;
    char  vehno[ 10 ] ;
    int  dist ;
} ;
struct  employee  e ;
```

Though grammatically there is nothing wrong with this structure, it suffers from a disadvantage. For any employee, depending upon his/her grade, either the fields hobby and credit card no. or the fields vehicle number and distance would get used. Both sets of fields would never get used. This would lead to wastage of memory with every structure variable that we create, since every structure variable would have all the four fields apart from name, grade and age. This can be avoided by creating a **union** between these sets of fields. This is shown below.

```
struct  info1
```

```
{
    char  hobby[ 10 ] ;
    int  crcardno ;
} ;
struct  info2
{
    char  vehno[ 10 ] ;
    int  dist ;
} ;
union  info
{
    struct  info1 a ;
    struct  info2  b ;
} ;
struct  employee
{
    char  n[ 20 ] ;
    char  grade[ 4 ] ;
    int  age ;
    union  info  f ;
} ;
struct  employee  e ;
```

Enumerated Data Type

The enumerated data type gives you an opportunity to invent your own data type and define what values the variable of this data type can take. This can help in making the program listings more readable, which can be an advantage when a program gets complicated or when more than one programmer would be working on it. Using enumerated data type can also help you reduce programming errors.

As an example, one could invent a data type called **mar_status** which can have four possible values—single, married, divorced or widowed. Don't confuse these values with variable names; married, for instance, has the same relationship to the variable **mar_status** as the number 15 has with a variable of type **int**.

The format of the **enum** definition is similar to that of a structure. Here's how the example stated above can be implemented.

```
enum  mar_status
{
```

single, married, divorced, widowed
```
};
enum mar_status person1, person2 ;
```

Like structures, this declaration has two parts:

(a) The first part declares the data type and specifies its possible values. These values are called 'enumerators'.

(b) The second part declares variables of this data type.

Now we can give values to these variables:

```
person1 = married ;
person2 = divorced ;
```

Remember, we can't use values that aren't in the original declaration.

Thus, the following expression would cause an error:

```
person1 = unknown ;
```

Internally, the compiler treats the enumerators as integers. Each value on the list of permissible values corresponds to an integer, starting with 0. Thus, in our example, single is stored as 0, married is stored as 1, divorced as 2 and widowed as 3.

This way of assigning numbers can be overridden by the programmer by initializing the enumerators to different integer values as shown below.

```
enum mar_status
{
    single = 100, married = 200, divorced = 300, widowed = 400
};
enum mar_status person1, person2 ;
```

Uses of Enumerated Data Type

Enumerated variables are usually used to clarify the operation of a program. For example, if we need to use employee departments in a payroll program, it makes the listing easier to read if we use values like Assembly, Manufacturing, Accounts rather than the integer values 0, 1, 2, etc. The following program illustrates the point I am trying to make:

```
# include <stdio.h>
# include <string.h>
```

```
int main( )
{
    enum emp_dept
    {
        assembly, manufacturing, accounts, stores
    } ;
    struct employee
    {
        char name[ 30 ] ;
        int age ;
        float bs ;
        enum emp_dept department ;
    } ;
    struct employee e ;

    strcpy ( e.name, "Lothar Mattheus" ) ;
    e.age = 28 ;
    e.bs = 5575.50 ;
    e.department = manufacturing ;

    printf ( "Name = %s\n", e.name ) ;
    printf ( "Age = %d\n", e.age ) ;
    printf ( "Basic salary = %f\n", e.bs ) ;
    printf ( "Dept = %d\n", e.department ) ;

    if ( e.department == accounts )
        printf ( "%s is an accounant\n", e.name ) ;
    else
        printf ( "%s is not an accounant\n", e.name ) ;
    return 0 ;
}
```

And here is the output of the program...

```
Name = Lothar Mattheus
Age = 28
Basic salary = 5575.50
Dept = 1
Lothar Mattheus is not an accountant
```

Let us now dissect the program. We first defined the data type **enum emp_dept** and specified the four possible values, namely, assembly, manufacturing, accounts and stores. Then we defined a variable **department** of the type **enum emp_dept** in a structure. The structure **employee** has three other elements containing employee information.

The program first assigns values to the variables in the structure. The statement,

e.department = manufacturing ;

assigns the value manufacturing to **e.department** variable. This is much more informative to anyone reading the program than a statement like,

e.department = 1 ;

The next part of the program shows an important weakness of using **enum** variables... there is no way to use the enumerated values directly in input/output functions like **scanf( )** and **printf( )**.

The **printf( )** function is not smart enough to perform the translation; the department is printed out as 1 and not manufacturing. Of course, we can write a function to print the correct enumerated values, using a **switch** statement, but that would reduce the clarity of the program. Even with this limitation, however, there are many situations in which enumerated variables are god sent!

Are Enums Necessary?

Is there a way to achieve what was achieved using Enums in the previous program? Yes, using macros as shown below.

```
# include <string.h>
# define ASSEMBLY 0
# define MANUFACTURING 1
# define ACCCOUNTS 2
# define STORES 3

int main( )
{
    struct employee
    {
        char name[ 30 ] ;
        int age ;
        float bs ;
        int department ;
```

```
    } ;
    struct employee e ;
    strcpy ( e.name, "Lothar Mattheus" ) ;
    e.age = 28 ;
    e.bs = 5575.50 ;
    e.department = MANUFACTURING ;
    return 0 ;
}
```

If the same effect—convenience and readability can be achieved using macros then why should we prefer enums? Because, macros have a global scope, whereas, scope of enum can either be global (if declared outside all functions) or local (if declared inside a function).

Exercise

[A] What will be the output of the following programs:

(a)
```c
# include <stdio.h>
int main( )
{
    int  num[ 26 ], temp ;
    num[ 0 ] = 100 ;
    num[ 25 ] = 200 ;
    temp = num[ 25 ] ;
    num[ 25 ] = num[ 0 ] ;
    num[ 0 ] = temp ;
    printf ( "%d %d\n", num[ 0 ], num[ 25 ] ) ;
    return 0 ;
}
```

(b)
```c
# include <stdio.h>
int main( )
{
    int  array[ 26 ], i ;
    for ( i = 0 ; i <= 25 ; i++ )
    {
        array[ i ] = 'A' + i ;
        printf ( "%d %c\n", array[ i ], array[ i ] ) ;
    }
    return 0 ;
}
```

(c)
```c
# include <stdio.h>
int main( )
{
    int  sub[ 50 ], i ;
    for ( i = 0 ; i <= 48 ; i++ ) ;
    {
        sub[ i ] = i ;
        printf ( "%d\n", sub[ i ] ) ;
    }
    return 0 ;
}
```

(d)
```c
# include <stdio.h>
int main( )
```

```
    {
        enum  status { pass, fail, atkt } ;
        enum  status  stud1, stud2, stud3 ;
        stud1 = pass ;
        stud2 = fail ;
        stud3 = atkt ;
        printf ( "%d %d %d\n", stud1, stud2, stud3 ) ;
        return 0 ;
    }
```

[B] Point out the errors, if any, in the following program segments:

(a)
```
    /* mixed has some char and some int values */
    # include <stdio.h>
    int char  mixed[ 100 ] ;
    int main( )
    {
        int a[ 10 ], i ;
        for ( i = 1 ; i <= 10 ; i++ )
        {
            scanf ( "%d", a[ i ] ) ;
            printf ( "%d\n", a[ i ] ) ;
        }
        return 0 ;
    }
```

(b)
```
    # include <stdio.h>
    int main( )
    {
        int  size ;
        scanf ( "%d", &size ) ;
        int arr[ size ] ;
        for ( i = 1 ; i <= size ; i++ )
        {
            scanf ( "%d", &arr[ i ] ) ;
            printf ( "%d\n", arr[ i ] ) ;
        }
        return 0 ;
    }
```

(c)
```
    # include <stdio.h>
    int main( )
```

```
{
    int i, a = 2, b = 3 ;
    int arr[ 2 + 3 ] ;
    for ( i = 0 ; i < a+b ; i++ )
    {
        scanf ( "%d", &arr[ i ] ) ;
        printf ( "%d\n", arr[ i ] ) ;
    }
    return 0 ;
}
```

(d)
```
# include <stdio.h>
int main( )
{
    int  three[ 3 ][ ] = {
                        2, 4, 3,
                        6, 8, 2,
                        2, 3, 1
                    } ;
    printf ( "%d\n", three[ 1 ][ 1 ] ) ;
    return 0 ;
}
```

(e)
```
# include <stdio.h>
# include <string.h>
int main( )
{
    struct  employee
    {
        char  name[ 25 ] ;
        int  age ;
        float  salary ;
    } ;
    struct  employee  e ;
    strcpy ( e.name, "Shailesh" ) ;
    age = 25 ;
    salary = 15500.00 ;
    printf ( "%s %d %f\n", e.name, age, salary ) ;
    return 0 ;
}
```

[C] Attempt the following:

(a) Twenty-five numbers are entered from the keyboard into an array. The number to be searched is entered through the keyboard by the user. Write a program to find if the number to be searched is present in the array and if it is present, display the number of times it appears in the array.

(b) Write a program to pick up the largest number from any 5 row by 5 column matrix.

(c) Write a program to obtain transpose of a 4 x 4 matrix. The transpose of a matrix is obtained by exchanging the elements of each row with the elements of the corresponding column.

(d) Write a program to find if a square matrix is symmetric.

(e) Write a program to add two 6 x 6 matrices.

(f) Write a program to multiply any two 3 x 3 matrices.

(g) The **X** and **Y** coordinates of 10 different points are entered through the keyboard. Write a program to find the distance of last point from the first point (sum of distances between consecutive points).

(h) Create a structure to specify data on students given below:

Roll number, Name, Department, Course, Year of joining

Assume that there are not more than 450 students in the college.

(1) Write a function to print names of all students who joined in a particular year.

(2) Write a function to print the data of a student whose roll number is received by the function.

(i) Create a structure to specify data of customers in a bank. The data to be stored is: Account number, Name, Balance in account. Assume maximum of 200 customers in the bank.

(1) Write a function to print the Account number and name of each customer with balance below Rs. 100.

(2) If a customer requests for withdrawal or deposit, the form contains the fields:

Acct. no, amount, code (1 for deposit, 0 for withdrawal)

Write a program to give a message, "The balance is insufficient for the specified withdrawal", if on withdrawal the balance falls below Rs. 100.

(j) An automobile company has serial number for engine parts starting from AA0 to FF9. The other characteristics of parts are year of manufacture, material and quantity manufactured.

(1) Specify a structure to store information corresponding to a part.

(2) Write a program to retrieve information on parts with serial numbers between BB1 and CC6.

Unit 5

Pointers

- Call by Value and Call by Reference
- An Introduction to Pointers
- Pointer Notation
- Back to Function Calls
- Conclusions
- File Handling
- Data Organization
- File Operations
  Opening a File
  Reading from a File
  Trouble in Opening a File
  Closing the File
- Counting Characters, Tabs, Spaces, ...
- A File-Copy Program
- String (Line) I/O in Files
- Record I/O in Files
- C Preprocessor
- Features of C Preprocessor
- Macro Expansion
  Macros with Arguments
- File Inclusion
- Conditional Compilation
- Command-line Arguments
- Exercise

Which feature of C do beginners find most difficult to understand? The answer is easy: pointers. Other languages have pointers but few use them so frequently as C does. And why not? It is C's clever use of pointers that makes it the excellent language it is. This chapter is devoted to pointers and their usage in function calls. Let us begin with the function calls.

Call by Value and Call by Reference

By now, we are well familiar with how to call functions. But, if you observe carefully, whenever we called a function and passed something to it we have always passed the 'values' of variables to the called function. Such function calls are called 'calls by value'. By this what we mean is, on calling a function, we are passing values of variables to it. The examples of call by value are shown below:

sum = calsum (a, b, c) ;
f = factr (a) ;

We have also learnt that variables are stored somewhere in memory. So instead of passing the value of a variable, can we not pass the location number (also called address) of the variable to a function? If we were able to do so, it would become a 'call by reference'. What purpose a 'call by reference' serves we would find out a little later. First we must equip ourselves with knowledge of how to make a 'call by reference'. This feature of C functions needs at least an elementary knowledge of a concept called 'pointers'. So let us first acquire the basics of pointers after which we would take up this topic once again.

An Introduction to Pointers

The difficulty beginners have with pointers has much to do with C's pointer terminology than the actual concept. For instance, when a C programmer says that a certain variable is a "pointer", what does that mean? It is hard to see how a variable can point to something, or in a certain direction.

It is hard to get a grip on pointers just by listening to programmer's jargon. In our discussion of C pointers, therefore, we will try to avoid this difficulty by explaining pointers in terms of programming concepts we already understand. The first thing we want to do is to explain the rationale of C's pointer notation.

Pointer Notation

Consider the declaration,

int i = 3 ;

This declaration tells the C compiler to:

(a)   Reserve space in memory to hold the integer value.

(b)   Associate the name i with this memory location.

(c)   Store the value 3 at this location.

We may represent i's location in memory by the memory map shown in Figure 5.1.

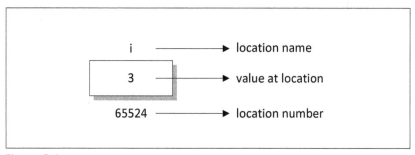

Figure 5.1

We see that the computer has selected memory location 65524 as the place to store the value 3. The location number 65524 is not a number to be relied upon, because some other time the computer may choose a different location for storing the value 3. The important point is, i's address in memory is a number.

We can print this address number through the following program:

```
# include <stdio.h>
int main( )
{
    int  i = 3 ;
    printf ( "Address of i = %u\n", &i ) ;
    printf ( "Value of i = %d\n", i ) ;
    return 0 ;
}
```

The output of the above program would be:

Address of i = 65524
Value of i = 3

Look at the first **printf( )** statement carefully. '&' used in this statement is C's 'address of' operator. The expression **&i** returns the address of the variable **i**, which in this case happens to be 65524. Since 65524 represents an address, there is no question of a sign being associated with it. Hence it is printed out using **%u**, which is a format specifier for printing an unsigned integer. We have been using the '&' operator all the time in the **scanf( )** statement.

The other pointer operator available in C is '*', called 'value at address' operator. It gives the value stored at a particular address. The 'value at address' operator is also called 'indirection' operator.

Observe carefully the output of the following program:

```
# include <stdio.h>
int main( )
{
    int  i = 3 ;
    printf ( "Address of i = %u\n", &i ) ;
    printf ( "Value of i = %d\n", i ) ;
    printf ( "Value of i = %d\n", *( &i ) ) ;
    return 0 ;
}
```

The output of the above program would be:

Address of i = 65524
Value of i = 3
Value of i = 3

Note that printing the value of ***(&i)** is same as printing the value of **i**.

The expression **&i** gives the address of the variable **i**. This address can be collected in a variable, by saying,

j = &i ;

But remember that **j** is not an ordinary variable like any other integer variable. It is a variable that contains the address of other variable (**i** in this case). Since **j** is a variable, the compiler must provide it space in the memory. Once again, the memory map shown in Figure 5.2 would illustrate the contents of **i** and **j**.

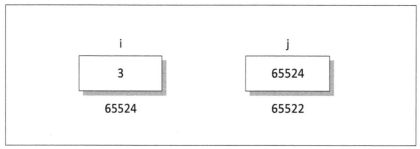

Figure 5.2

As you can see, **i**'s value is 3 and **j**'s value is **i**'s address.

But wait, we can't use **j** in a program without declaring it. And since **j** is a variable that contains the address of **i**, it is declared as,

int *j ;

This declaration tells the compiler that **j** will be used to store the address of an integer value. In other words, **j** points to an integer. How do we justify the usage of * in the declaration,

int *j ;

Let us go by the meaning of *. It stands for 'value at address'. Thus, **int *j** would mean, the value at the address contained in **j** is an **int**.

Here is a program that demonstrates the relationships we have been discussing.

```
# include <stdio.h>
int main( )
{
    int i = 3 ;
    int *j ;

    j = &i ;
    printf ( "Address of i = %u\n", &i ) ;
    printf ( "Address of i = %u\n", j ) ;
    printf ( "Address of j = %u\n", &j ) ;
    printf ( "Value of j = %u\n", j ) ;
    printf ( "Value of i = %d\n", i ) ;
```

```
    printf ( "Value of i = %d\n", *( &i ) ) ;
    printf ( "Value of i = %d\n", *j ) ;
    return 0 ;
}
```

The output of the above program would be:

Address of i = 65524
Address of i = 65524
Address of j = 65522
Value of j = 65524
Value of i = 3
Value of i = 3
Value of i = 3

Work through the above program carefully, taking help of the memory locations of **i** and **j** shown earlier. This program summarizes everything that we have discussed so far. If you don't understand the program's output, or the meanings of **&i, &j, *j** and ***(&i)**, re-read the last few pages. Everything we say about pointers from here onwards will depend on your understanding these expressions thoroughly.

Look at the following declarations:

```
int *alpha ;
char *ch ;
float *s ;
```

Here, **alpha, ch** and **s** are declared as pointer variables, i.e., variables capable of holding addresses. Remember that, addresses (location nos.) are always going to be whole numbers, therefore pointers always contain whole numbers. Now we can put these two facts together and say—pointers are variables that contain addresses, and since addresses are always whole numbers, pointers would always contain whole numbers.

The declaration **float *s** does not mean that **s** is going to contain a floating-point value. What it means is, **s** is going to contain the address of a floating-point value. Similarly, **char *ch** means that **ch** is going to contain the address of a char value. Or in other words, the value at address stored in **ch** is going to be a **char**.

The concept of pointers can be further extended. Pointer, we know is a variable that contains address of another variable. Now this variable itself might be another pointer. Thus, we now have a pointer that contains another pointer's address. The following example should make this point clear:

```
# include <stdio.h>
int main( )
{
    int  i = 3, *j, **k ;

    j = &i ;
    k = &j ;
    printf ( "Address of i = %u\n", &i ) ;
    printf ( "Address of i = %u\n ", j ) ;
    printf ( "Address of i = %u\n ", *k ) ;
    printf ( "Address of j = %u\n ", &j ) ;
    printf ( "Address of j = %u\n ", k ) ;
    printf ( "Address of k = %u\n ", &k ) ;
    printf ( "Value of j  = %u\n ", j ) ;
    printf ( "Value of k  = %u\n ", k ) ;
    printf ( "Value of i  = %d\n ", i ) ;
    printf ( "Value of i  = %d\n ", * ( &i ) ) ;
    printf ( "Value of i  = %d\n ", *j ) ;
    printf ( "Value of i  = %d\n ", **k ) ;
    return 0 ;
}
```

The output of the above program would be:

Address of i = 65524
Address of i = 65524
Address of i = 65524
Address of j = 65522
Address of j = 65522
Address of k = 65520
Value of j = 65524
Value of k = 65522
Value of i = 3
Value of i = 3
Value of i = 3
Value of i = 3

Figure 5.3 would help you in tracing out how the program prints the above output.

Remember that when you run this program, the addresses that get printed might turn out to be something different than the ones shown in Figure 5.3. However, with these addresses too, the relationship between **i, j** and **k** can be easily established.

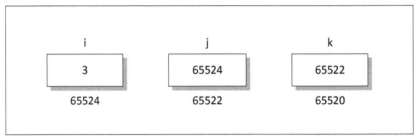

Figure 5.3

Observe how the variables **j** and **k** have been declared,

int i, *j, **k ;

Here, **i** is an ordinary **int**, **j** is a pointer to an **int** (often called an integer pointer), whereas **k** is a pointer to an integer pointer. We can extend the above program still further by creating a pointer to a pointer to an integer pointer. In principle, you would agree that likewise there could exist a pointer to a pointer to a pointer to a pointer to a pointer. There is no limit on how far can we go on extending this definition. Possibly, till the point we can comprehend it. And that point of comprehension is usually a pointer to a pointer. Beyond this, one rarely requires to extend the definition of a pointer. But just in case...

Back to Function Calls

Having had the first tryst with pointers, let us now get back to what we had originally set out to learn—the two types of function calls—call by value and call by reference. Arguments can generally be passed to functions in one of the two ways:

(a) sending the values of the arguments

(b) sending the addresses of the arguments

In the first method, the 'value' of each of the actual arguments in the calling function is copied into corresponding formal arguments of the called function. With this method, the changes made to the formal arguments in the called function have no effect on the values of actual arguments in the calling function. The following program illustrates the 'Call by Value':

```
# include <stdio.h>
void swapv ( int  x, int  y ) ;
int main( )
{
    int  a = 10, b = 20 ;
    swapv ( a, b ) ;
    printf ( "a = %d b = %d\n", a, b ) ;
    return 0 ;
}
void swapv ( int  x, int  y )
{
    int  t ;
    t = x ;
    x = y ;
    y = t ;
    printf ( "x = %d y = %d\n", x, y ) ;
}
```

The output of the above program would be:

```
x = 20 y = 10
a = 10 b = 20
```

Note that values of **a** and **b** remain unchanged even after exchanging the values of **x** and **y**.

In the second method (call by reference), the addresses of actual arguments in the calling function are copied into the formal arguments of the called function. This means that, using these addresses, we would have an access to the actual arguments and hence we would be able to manipulate them. The following program illustrates this fact:

```
# include <stdio.h>
void swapr ( int  *, int  * ) ;
int main( )
{
    int  a = 10, b = 20 ;
    swapr ( &a, &b ) ;
```

```
    printf ( "a = %d b = %d\n", a, b ) ;
    return 0 ;
}
void swapr ( int *x, int *y )
{
    int t ;

    t = *x ;
    *x = *y ;
    *y = t ;
}
```

The output of the above program would be:

a = 20 b = 10

Note that this program manages to exchange the values of **a** and **b** using their addresses stored in **x** and **y**.

Usually, in C programming, we make a call by value. This means that, in general, you cannot alter the actual arguments. But if desired, it can always be achieved through a call by reference.

Using a call by reference intelligently, we can make a function return more than one value at a time, which is not possible ordinarily. This is shown in the program given below.

```
# include <stdio.h>
void areaperi ( int, float *, float * ) ;
int main( )
{
    int  radius ;
    float  area, perimeter ;

    printf ( "Enter radius of a circle " ) ;
    scanf ( "%d", &radius ) ;
    areaperi ( radius, &area, &perimeter ) ;

    printf ( "Area = %f\n", area ) ;
    printf ( "Perimeter = %f\n", perimeter ) ;
    return 0 ;
}
void areaperi ( int  r, float *a, float *p )
```

```
{
    *a = 3.14 * r * r ;
    *p = 2 * 3.14 * r ;
}
```

And here is the output...

Enter radius of a circle 5
Area = 78.500000
Perimeter = 31.400000

Here, we are making a mixed call, in the sense, we are passing the value of **radius** but, addresses of **area** and **perimeter**. And since we are passing the addresses, any change that we make in values stored at addresses contained in the variables **a** and **p**, would make the change effective in **main( )**. That is why, when the control returns from the function **areaperi( )**, we are able to output the values of **area** and **perimeter**.

Thus, we have been able to indirectly return two values from a called function, and hence, have overcome the limitation of the **return** statement, which can return only one value from a function at a time.

Conclusions

From the programs that we discussed here, we can draw the following conclusions:

(a) If we want that the value of an actual argument should not get changed in the function being called, pass the actual argument by value.

(b) If we want that the value of an actual argument should get changed in the function being called, pass the actual argument by reference.

(c) If a function is to be made to return more than one value at a time, then return these values indirectly by using a call by reference.

File Handling

Often it is not enough to just display the data on the screen. This is because if the data is large, only a limited amount of it can be stored in memory and only a limited amount of it can be displayed on the screen. It would be inappropriate to store this data in memory for one more reason. Memory is volatile and its contents would be lost once the program is terminated. So if we need the same data again it would have to be either entered through the keyboard again or would have to be regenerated programmatically. Obviously both these operations would be tedious. At such times it becomes necessary to store the data in a manner that can be later retrieved and displayed either in part or in whole. This medium is usually a 'file' on the disk. Let us see how file I/O (Input/Output) operations can be performed.

Data Organization

Before we start doing file input/output let us first find out how data is organized on the disk. All data stored on the disk is in binary form. How this binary data is stored on the disk varies from one OS to another. However, this does not affect the C programmer since he has to use only the library functions written for the particular OS to be able to perform input/output. It is the compiler vendor's responsibility to correctly implement these library functions by taking the help of OS. This is illustrated in Figure 5.4.

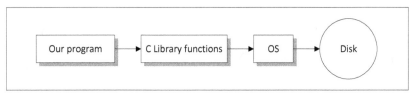

Figure 5.4

File Operations

There are different operations that can be carried out on a file. These are:

(a) Creation of a new file
(b) Opening an existing file
(c) Reading from a file
(d) Writing to a file
(e) Moving to a specific location in a file (seeking)
(f) Closing a file

Let us now write a program to read a file and display its contents on the screen. We will first list the program and show what it does, and then dissect it line-by-line. Here is the listing...

```
/* Display contents of a file on screen. */
# include <stdio.h>
int main( )
```

```
{
    FILE *fp ;
    char ch ;

    fp = fopen ( "PR1.C", "r" ) ;
    while ( 1 )
    {
        ch = fgetc ( fp ) ;
        if ( ch == EOF )
            break ;

        printf ( "%c", ch ) ;
    }
    printf ( "\n" ) ;
    fclose ( fp ) ;
    return 0 ;
}
```

On execution of this program it displays the contents of the file 'PR1.C' on the screen. Let us now understand how it does the same.

Opening a File

Before we can read (or write) information from (to) a file on a disk we must open the file. To open the file we have called the function **fopen( )**. It would open a file "**PR1.C**" in '**read**' mode, which tells the C compiler that we would be reading the contents of the file. Note that "**r**" is a string and not a character; hence the double quotes and not single quotes. In fact **fopen( )** performs three important tasks when you open the file in "**r**" mode:

(a) Firstly it searches on the disk the file to be opened.
(b) Then it loads the file from the disk into a place in memory called buffer.
(c) It sets up a character pointer that points to the first character of the buffer.

Why do we need a buffer at all? Imagine how inefficient it would be to actually access the disk every time we want to read a character from it. Every time we read something from a disk, it takes some time for the disk drive to position the read/write head correctly. On a floppy disk system, the drive motor has to actually start rotating the disk from a standstill position every time the disk is accessed. If this were to be done for every character we read from the disk, it would take a long time to complete the reading operation. This is where a buffer comes in. It would be more sensible to read the contents of the file into the buffer while opening the file and then read the file character by character from the buffer rather than from the disk. This is shown in Figure 5.5.

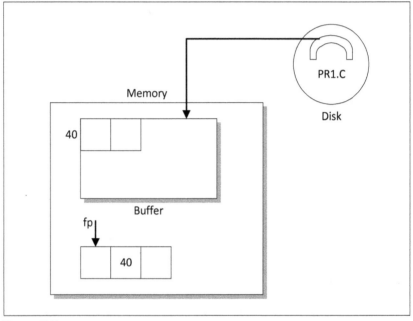

Figure 5.5

Same argument also applies to writing information in a file. Instead of writing characters in the file on the disk one character at a time it would be more efficient to write characters in a buffer and then finally transfer the contents from the buffer to the disk.

To be able to successfully read from a file, information like mode of opening, size of file, place in the file from where the next read operation would be performed, etc., has to be maintained. Since all this information is inter-related, all of it is gathered together by **fopen( )** in a structure called **FILE**. **fopen( )** returns the address of this structure, which we have collected in the structure pointer called **fp**. We have declared **fp** as follows:

FILE *fp ;

The **FILE** structure has been defined in the header file "stdio.h" (standing for standard input/output header file). Therefore, it is necessary to **#include** this file.

Reading from a File

Once the file has been opened for reading using **fopen( )**, as we have seen, the file's contents are brought into buffer (partly or wholly) and a pointer is set up that points to the first character in the buffer. This pointer is one of the elements of the structure to which **fp** is pointing (refer Figure 5.5).

To read the file's contents from memory, there exists a function called **fgetc( )**. This has been used in our program as,

ch = fgetc (fp) ;

fgetc( ) reads the character from the current pointer position, advances the pointer position so that it now points to the next character, and returns the character that is read, which we collected in the variable **ch**. Note that once the file has been opened, we no longer refer to the file by its name, but through the file pointer **fp**.

We have used the function **fgetc( )** within an indefinite **while** loop. There has to be a way to break out of this **while**. When shall we break out... when all the characters from the file have been read. But how would we know this? Well, **fgetc( )** returns a macro EOF (End of File) once all the characters have been read and we attempt to read one more character. The EOF macro has been defined in the file "stdio.h". In place of the function **fgetc( )**, we could have as well used the macro **getc( )** with the same effect.

In our program we go on reading each character from the file till end of file is not met. As each character is read, we display it on the screen. Once out of the loop, we close the file.

Trouble in Opening a File

There is a possibility that when we try to open a file using the function **fopen( )**, the file may not be opened. While opening the file in "**r**" mode, this may happen because the file being opened may not be present on the disk at all. And you obviously cannot read a file that doesn't exist. Similarly, while opening the file for writing, **fopen( )** may fail due to a number of reasons, like, disk space may be insufficient to create a new file, or the disk may be write protected or the disk is damaged and so on.

Crux of the matter is that it is important for any program that accesses disk files to check whether a file has been opened successfully before trying to read or write to the file. If the file opening fails due to any of the several reasons mentioned above, the **fopen( )** function returns a value NULL (defined in "stdio.h" as **#define NULL 0**). Here is how this can be handled in a program...

```
# include <stdio.h>
# include <stdlib.h>
int main( )
{
    FILE *fp ;
    fp = fopen ( "PR1.C", "r" ) ;
    if ( fp == NULL )
    {
        puts ( "cannot open file" ) ;
        exit ( 1 ) ;
    }
    return 0 ;
}
```

The call to the function **exit( )** terminates the execution of the program. Usually, a value 0 is passed to **exit( )** if the program termination is normal. A non-zero value indicates an abnormal termination of the program. If there are multiple exit points in the program, then the value passed to **exit( )** can be used to find out from where the execution of the program got terminated. There are different ways of examining this value in different programming environments. For example, in Visual Studio this value is shown in the Output Window at the bottom. In Turbo C++ this value can be seen through the Compile | Information menu item. The prototype of **exit( )** function is declared in the header file **stdlib.h**.

Closing the File

When we have finished reading from the file, we need to close it. This is done using the function **fclose( )** through the statement,

fclose (fp) ;

Once we close the file, we can no longer read from it using **getc( )** unless we reopen the file. Note that to close the file, we don't use the filename but the file pointer **fp**. On closing the file, the buffer associated with the file is removed from memory.

In this program we have opened the file for reading. Suppose we open a file with an intention to write characters into it. This time too, a buffer would get associated with it. When we attempt to write characters into this file using **fputc( )** the characters would get written to the buffer. When we close this file using **fclose( )** two operations would be performed:

(a) The characters in the buffer would be written to the file on the disk.
(b) The buffer would be eliminated from memory.

You can imagine a possibility when the buffer may become full before we close the file. In such a case the buffer's contents would be written to the disk the moment it becomes full. All this buffer management is done for us by the library functions.

Counting Characters, Tabs, Spaces, ...

Having understood the first file I/O program in detail let us now try our hand at one more. Let us write a program that will read a file and count how many characters, spaces, tabs and newlines are present in it. Here is the program...

```
/* Count chars, spaces, tabs and newlines in a file */
# include <stdio.h>
int main( )
{
    FILE  *fp ;
    char  ch ;
    int  nol = 0, not = 0, nob = 0, noc = 0 ;

    fp = fopen ( "PR1.C", "r" ) ;
    while ( 1 )
    {
        ch = fgetc ( fp ) ;
        if ( ch == EOF )
            break ;
        noc++ ;
        if ( ch == ' ' )
            nob++ ;
```

```
        if ( ch == '\n' )
             nol++ ;
        if ( ch == '\t' )
             not++ ;
    }
    fclose ( fp ) ;
    printf ( "Number of characters = %d\n", noc ) ;
    printf ( "Number of blanks = %d\n", nob ) ;
    printf ( "Number of tabs = %d\n", not ) ;
    printf ( "Number of lines = %d\n", nol ) ;
    return 0 ;
}
```

Here is a sample run...

```
Number of characters = 125
Number of blanks = 25
Number of tabs = 13
Number of lines = 22
```

The above statistics are true for a file "PR1.C", which I had on my disk. You may give any other filename and obtain different results. I believe the program is self-explanatory.

In this program too, we have opened the file for reading and then read it character-by-character. Let us now try a program that needs to open a file for writing.

A File-Copy Program

We have already used the function **fgetc( )** which reads characters from a file. Its counterpart is a function called **fputc( )** which writes characters to a file. As a practical use of these character I/O functions, we can copy the contents of one file into another, as demonstrated in the following program. This program takes the contents of a file and copies them into another file, character-by-character.

```
# include <stdio.h>
# include <stdlib.h>
int main( )
{
    FILE *fs, *ft ;
    char ch ;
```

```
fs = fopen ( "pr1.c", "r" ) ;
if ( fs == NULL )
{
    puts ( "Cannot open source file" ) ;
    exit ( 1 ) ;
}
ft = fopen ( "pr2.c", "w" ) ;
if ( ft == NULL )
{
    puts ( "Cannot open target file" ) ;
    fclose ( fs ) ;
    exit ( 2 ) ;
}
while ( 1 )
{
    ch = fgetc ( fs ) ;

    if ( ch == EOF )
        break ;
    else
        fputc ( ch, ft ) ;
}
fclose ( fs ) ;
fclose ( ft ) ;
return 0 ;
}
```

I hope most of the stuff in the program can be easily understood, since it has already been dealt with in the earlier section. What is new is only the function **fputc( )**. Let us see how it works.

Writing to a File

The **fputc( )** function is similar to the **putch( )** function, in the sense that both output characters. However, **putch( )** function always writes to the VDU, whereas, **fputc( )** writes to the file. Which file? The file signified by **ft**. The writing process continues till all characters from the source file have been written to the target file, following which the **while** loop terminates.

Note that our sample file-copy program is capable of copying only text files. To copy files with extension .EXE or .JPG, we need to open the files in binary mode.

String (Line) I/O in Files

For many purposes, character I/O is just what is needed. However, in some situations, the usage of functions that read or write entire strings might turn out to be more efficient.

Reading or writing strings of characters from and to files is as easy as reading and writing individual characters. Here is a program that writes strings to a file using the function **fputs( )**.

```
/* Receives strings from keyboard and writes them to file */
# include <stdio.h>
# include <stdlib.h>
# include <string.h>
int main( )
{
    FILE  *fp ;
    char  s[ 80 ] ;

    fp = fopen ( "POEM.TXT", "w" ) ;
    if ( fp == NULL )
    {
        puts ( "Cannot open file" ) ;
        exit ( 1 ) ;
    }
    printf ( "\nEnter a few lines of text:\n" ) ;
    while ( strlen ( gets ( s ) ) > 0 )
    {
        fputs ( s, fp ) ;
        fputs ( "\n", fp ) ;
    }
    fclose ( fp ) ;
    return 0 ;
}
```

And here is a sample run of the program...

Enter a few lines of text:
Shining and bright, they are forever,

so true about diamonds,
more so of memories,
especially yours!

Note that each string is terminated by hitting Enter. To terminate the execution of the program, hit Enter at the beginning of a line. This creates a string of zero length, which the program recognizes as the signal to close the file and exit.

We have set up a character array to receive the string; the **fputs( )** function then writes the contents of the array to the disk. Since **fputs( )** does not automatically add a newline character to the end of the string, we must do this explicitly to make it easier to read the string back from the file.

Here is a program that reads strings from a disk file.

```c
/* Reads strings from the file and displays them on screen */
# include <stdio.h>
# include <stdlib.h>
int main( )
{
    FILE *fp ;
    char  s[ 80 ] ;

    fp = fopen ( "POEM.TXT", "r" ) ;
    if ( fp == NULL )
    {
        puts ( "Cannot open file" ) ;
        exit ( 1 ) ;
    }

    while ( fgets ( s, 79, fp ) != NULL )
        printf ( "%s" , s ) ;

    printf ( "\n" ) ;
    fclose ( fp ) ;
    return 0 ;
}
```

And here is the output...

Shining and bright, they are forever,

so true about diamonds,
more so of memories,
especially yours !

The function **fgets( )** takes three arguments. The first is the address where the string is stored, and the second is the maximum length of the string. This argument prevents **fgets( )** from reading in too long a string and overflowing the array. The third argument, as usual, is the pointer to the structure **FILE**. On reading a line from the file, the string **s** would contain the line contents a '\n' followed by a '\0'. Thus the string is terminated by **fgets( )** and we do not have to terminate it specifically. When all the lines from the file have been read, we attempt to read one more line, in which case **fgets( )** returns a **NULL**.

Record I/O in Files

So far, we have dealt with reading and writing only characters and strings. What if we want to read or write numbers from/to file? Furthermore, what if we desire to read/write a combination of characters, strings and numbers? For this first we would organize this dissimilar data together in a structure and then use **fprintf( )** and **fscanf( )** library functions to read/write data from/to file. Following program illustrates the use of structures for writing records of employees:

```
/* Writes records to a file using structure */
# include <stdio.h>
# include <conio.h>
int main( )
{
    FILE *fp ;
    char another = 'Y' ;
    struct emp
    {
        char name[ 40 ] ;
        int age ;
        float bs ;
    } ;
    struct emp e ;

    fp = fopen ( "EMPLOYEE.DAT", "w" ) ;
```

```
    if ( fp == NULL )
    {
        puts ( "Cannot open file" ) ;
        exit ( 1 ) ;
    }

    while ( another == 'Y' )
    {
        printf ( "\nEnter name, age and basic salary: " ) ;
        scanf ( "%s %d %f", e.name, &e.age, &e.bs ) ;
        fprintf ( fp, "%s %d %f\n", e.name, e.age, e.bs ) ;

        printf ( "Add another record (Y/N) " ) ;
        fflush ( stdin ) ;
        another = getche( ) ;
    }

    fclose ( fp ) ;
    return 0 ;
}
```

And here is the output of the program...

Enter name, age and basic salary: Sunil 34 1250.50
Add another record (Y/N) Y
Enter name, age and basic salary: Sameer 21 1300.50
Add another record (Y/N) Y
Enter name, age and basic salary: Rahul 34 1400.55
Add another record (Y/N) N

In this program we are just reading the data into a structure variable using **scanf( )**, and then dumping it into a disk file using **fprintf( )**. The user can input as many records as he/she desires. The procedure ends when the user supplies 'N' for the question 'Add another record (Y/N)'.

The key to this program is the function **fprintf( )**, which writes the values in the structure variable to the file. This function is similar to **printf( )**, except that a **FILE** pointer is included as the first argument. As in **printf( )**, we can format the data in a variety of ways, by using **fprintf( )**. In fact, all the format conventions of **printf( )** function work with **fprintf( )** as well.

Perhaps you are wondering what for have we used the function **fflush( )**. The reason is to get rid of a peculiarity of **scanf( )**. After supplying data for one employee, we would hit the Enter key. What **scanf( )** does is it assigns name, age and salary to appropriate variables and keeps the Enter key unread in the keyboard buffer. So when it's time to supply Y or N for the question 'Another employee (Y/N)', **getch( )** will read the Enter key from the buffer thinking that user has entered the Enter key. To avoid this problem, we use the function **fflush( )**. It is designed to remove or 'flush out' any data remaining in the buffer. The argument to **fflush( )** must be the buffer which we want to flush out. Here we have used 'stdin', which means buffer related with standard input device— keyboard.

Let us now write a program that reads the employee records created by the above program. Here is how it can be done...

```c
/* Read records from a file using structure */
# include <stdio.h>
# include <stdlib.h>
int main( )
{
    FILE *fp ;
    struct emp
    {
        char  name[ 40 ] ;
        int  age ;
        float  bs ;
    } ;
    struct emp  e ;

    fp = fopen ( "EMPLOYEE.DAT", "r" ) ;

    if ( fp == NULL )
    {
        puts ( "Cannot open file" ) ;
        exit ( 1 ) ;
    }

    while ( fscanf ( fp, "%s %d %f", e.name, &e.age, &e.bs ) != EOF )
        printf ( "%s %d %f\n", e.name, e.age, e.bs ) ;

    fclose ( fp ) ;
```

```
    return 0 ;
}
```

And here is the output of the program...

```
Sunil 34 1250.500000
Sameer 21 1300.500000
Rahul 34 1400.500000
```

C Preprocessor

The C preprocessor is exactly what its name implies. It is a program that processes our source program before it is passed to the compiler. Preprocessor commands (often known as directives) form what can almost be considered a language within C language. We can certainly write C programs without knowing anything about the preprocessor or its facilities. But preprocessor is such a great convenience that virtually all C programmers rely on it. Let us now explore the preprocessor directives, and discuss the pros and cons of using them in programs.

Features of C Preprocessor

Bbefore a C program is compiled it is passed through another program called 'Preprocessor'. The C program is often known as 'Source Code'. The Preprocessor works on the source code and creates 'Expanded Source Code'. If the source code is stored in a file PR1.C, then the expanded source code gets stored in a file PR1.I. It is this expanded source code that is sent to the compiler for compilation.

The preprocessor offers several features called preprocessor directives. Each of these preprocessor directives begins with a # symbol. The directives can be placed anywhere in a program but are most often placed at the beginning of a program, before the first function definition. We would learn the following preprocessor directives here:

(a) Macro expansion
(b) File inclusion
(c) Conditional compilation

Let us understand these features of preprocessor one-by-one.

Macro Expansion

Have a look at the following program:

```
# include <stdio.h>
```

```
# define UPPER 25
int main( )
{
    int i ;
    for ( i = 1 ; i <= UPPER ; i++ )
        printf ( "%d\n", i ) ;
    return 0 ;
}
```

In this program, instead of writing 25 in the **for** loop we are writing it in the form of UPPER, which has already been defined before **main( )** through the statement,

```
# define UPPER 25
```

This statement is called 'macro definition' or more commonly, just a 'macro'. What purpose does it serve? During preprocessing, the preprocessor replaces every occurrence of UPPER in the program with 25. Here is another example of macro definition.

```
# include <stdio.h>
# define PI  3.1415
int main( )
{
    float  r = 6.25 ;
    float  area ;

    area = PI * r * r ;
    printf ( "Area of circle = %f\n", area ) ;
    return 0 ;
}
```

UPPER and PI in the above programs are often called 'macro templates', whereas, 25 and 3.1415 are called their corresponding 'macro expansions'.

When we compile the program, before the source code passes to the compiler, it is examined by the C preprocessor for any macro definitions. When it sees the **#define** directive, it goes through the entire program in search of the macro templates; wherever it finds one, it replaces the macro template with the appropriate macro expansion. Only after this procedure has been completed, is the program handed over to the compiler.

In C programming, it is customary to use capital letters for macro template. This makes it easy for programmers to pick out all the macro templates when reading through the program.

Note that a macro template and its macro expansion are separated by blanks or tabs. A space between **#** and **define** is optional. Remember that a macro definition is never to be terminated by a semicolon.

Macros with Arguments

The macros that we have used so far are called simple macros. Macros can have arguments, just as functions can. Here is an example that illustrates this fact.

```
# include <stdio.h>
# define AREA(x) ( 3.14 * x * x )

int main( )
{
    float  r1 = 6.25, r2 = 2.5, a ;

    a = AREA ( r1 ) ;
    printf ( "Area of circle = %f\n", a ) ;
    a = AREA ( r2 ) ;
    printf ( "Area of circle = %f\n", a ) ;
    return 0 ;
}
```

Here's the output of the program...

```
Area of circle = 122.656250
Area of circle = 19.625000
```

In this program, wherever the preprocessor finds the phrase **AREA(x)** it expands it into the statement **(3.14 * x * x)**. However, that's not all that it does. The **x** in the macro template **AREA(x)** is an argument that matches the **x** in the macro expansion **(3.14 * x * x)**. The statement **AREA(r1)** in the program causes the variable **r1** to be substituted for **x**. Thus the statement **AREA(r1)** is equivalent to:

(3.14 * r1 * r1)

After the above source code has passed through the preprocessor, what the compiler gets to work on will be this:

```
# include <stdio.h>
int main( )
{
    float  r1 = 6.25, r2 = 2.5, a ;

    a = 3.14 * r1 *r1 ;
    printf ( "Area of circle = %f\n", a ) ;
    a = 3.14 *r2 * r2 ;
    printf ( "Area of circle = %f\n", a ) ;
    return 0 ;
}
```

Here is another example of macros with arguments:

```
# include <stdio.h>
# define ISDIGIT(y) ( y >= 48 && y <= 57 )

int main( )
{
    char  ch ;

    printf ( "Enter any digit " ) ;
    scanf ( "%c", &ch ) ;

    if ( ISDIGIT ( ch ) )
        printf ( "You entered a digit\n" ) ;
    else
        printf ( "Illegal input\n" ) ;
    return 0 ;
}
```

Here are some important points to remember while writing macros with arguments:

(a) Be careful not to leave a blank between the macro template and its argument while defining the macro. For example, there should be no blank between **AREA** and **(x)** in the definition, #define AREA(x) (3.14 * x * x)

If we were to write **AREA (x)** instead of **AREA(x)**, the **(x)** would become a part of macro expansion, which we certainly don't want. What would happen is, the template would be expanded to

(r1) (3.14 * r1 * r1)

which won't run. Not at all what we wanted.

(b) The entire macro expansion should be enclosed within parentheses. Here is an example of what would happen if we fail to enclose the macro expansion within parentheses.

```
# include <stdio.h>
# define SQUARE(n) n * n

int main( )
{
    int  j ;

    j = 64 / SQUARE ( 4 ) ;
    printf ( "j = %d\n", j ) ;
    return 0 ;
}
```

The output of the above program would be:

j = 64

whereas, what we expected was j = 4.

What went wrong? The macro was expanded into

j = 64 / 4 * 4 ;

which yielded 64.

File Inclusion

The second preprocessor directive we'll explore in this chapter is file inclusion. This directive causes one file to be included in another. The preprocessor command for file inclusion looks like this:

include "filename"

and it simply causes the entire contents of **filename** to be inserted into the source code at that point in the program. Of course, this presumes that the file being included exists. When and why this feature is used? It can be used in two cases:

(a) If we have a very large program, the code is best divided into several different files, each containing a set of related functions. It is a good programming practice to keep different sections of a large program separate. These files are **#included** at the beginning of main program file.

(b) There are some functions and some macro definitions that we need almost in all programs that we write. These commonly needed functions and macro definitions can be stored in a file, and that file can be included in every program we write, which would add all the statements in this file to our program as if we have typed them in.

(c) When creating our own library of functions which we wish to distribute to others. In this situation the functions are defined in a ".c" file and their corresponding prototype declarations and macros are declared in a ".h" file. While distributing the definitions are compiled into a library file (in machine language) and then the library file and the ".h" file. This way the function definitions in the ".c" file remain with you and are not exposed to users of these functions.

It is common for the files that are to be included to have a .h extension. This extension stands for 'header file', because it contains statements which when included go to the head of your program. The prototypes of all the library functions are grouped into different categories and then stored in different header files. For example, prototypes of all mathematics related functions are stored in the header file 'math.h', prototypes of console input/output functions are stored in the header file 'conio.h', and so on.

Actually there exist two ways to write **#include** statement. These are:

include "filename"
include <filename>

The meaning of each of these forms is given below.

include "mylib.h"   This command would look for the file **mylib.h** in the current directory as well as the specified list of directories as mentioned in the include search path that might have been set up.

include <mylib.h>   This command would look for the file **mylib.h** in the specified list of directories only.

The include search path is nothing but a list of directories that would be searched for the file being included. Different C compilers let you set the search path in different manners. If you are using Turbo C/C++ compiler, then the search path can be set up by selecting 'Directories' from the 'Options' menu. On doing this, a dialog box appears. In this dialog box against 'Include Directories', we can specify the search path. We can also specify multiple include paths separated by ';' (semicolon) as shown below.

c:\tc\lib ; c:\mylib ; d:\libfiles

The path can contain maximum of 127 characters. Both relative and absolute paths are valid. For example, '..\dir\incfiles' is a valid path.

In Visual Studio the search path for a project can be set by right-clicking the project name in Solution Explorer and selecting "Properties" from the menu that pops up. This brings up a dialog box. You can now set up the search path by going to "Include Directories" in "Configuration Properties" tab.

Conditional Compilation

We can, if we want, have the compiler skip over part of a source code by inserting the preprocessing commands **#ifdef** and **#endif**, which have the general form given below.

```
# ifdef  macroname
    statement 1 ;
    statement 2 ;
    statement 3 ;
# endif
```

If **macroname** has been **#defin**ed, the block of code will be processed as usual; otherwise not.

Where would **#ifdef** be useful? When would you like to compile only a part of your program? In three cases:

(a) To "comment out" obsolete lines of code. It often happens that a program is changed at the last minute to satisfy a client. This involves rewriting some part of source code to the client's satisfaction and deleting the old code. But veteran programmers are familiar with the clients who change their mind and want the old code back again just the way it was. Now you would definitely not like to retype the deleted code again.

One solution in such a situation is to put the old code within a pair of /* - - - */ combination. But we might have already written a comment in the code that we are about to "comment out". This would mean we end up with nested comments. Obviously, this solution won't work since we can't nest comments in C.

Therefore, the solution is to use conditional compilation as shown below.

```
int main( )
{
    # ifdef OKAY
        statement 1 ;
        statement 2 ;  /* detects virus */
        statement 3 ;
        statement 4 ;  /* specific to stone virus */
    # endif

    statement 5 ;
    statement 6 ;
    statement 7 ;
}
```

Here, statements 1, 2, 3 and 4 would get compiled only if the macro OKAY has been defined, and we have purposefully omitted the definition of the macro OKAY. At a later date, if we want that these statements should also get compiled, all that we are required to do is to delete the **#ifdef** and **#endif** statements.

(b) A more sophisticated use of **#ifdef** has to do with making the programs portable, i.e., to make them work on two totally different computers. Suppose an organization has two different types of computers and you are expected to write a program that works on both the machines. You can do so by isolating the lines of code that must be different for each machine by marking them off with **#ifdef**. For example:

```
int main( )
{
    # ifdef INTEL
```

```
        code suitable for an Intel PC
    # else
        code suitable for a Motorola PC
    # endif
    code common to both the computers
}
```

When you compile this program, it would compile only the code suitable for Mototola PC and the common code. This is because the macro INTEL has not been defined. Note that, the working of **#ifdef - #else - #endif** is similar to the ordinary **if - else** control instruction of C.

If you want to run your program on a Intel PC, just add a statement at the top saying,

define INTEL

Sometimes, instead of **#ifdef**, the **#ifndef** directive is used. The **#ifndef** (which means 'if not defined') works exactly opposite to **#ifdef**. The above example, if written using **#ifndef**, would look like this:

```
int main( )
{
    # ifndef INTEL
        code suitable for a Motorola PC
    # else
        code suitable for a Intel PC
    # endif
    code common to both the computers
}
```

(c) Suppose a function **myfunc( )** is defined in a file 'myfile.h' which is **#include**d in a file 'myfile1.h'. Now in your program file, if you **#include** both 'myfile.h' and 'myfile1.h', the compiler flashes an error 'Multiple declaration for **myfunc**'. This is because the same file 'myfile.h' gets included twice. To avoid this, we can write following code in the 'myfile.h' header file:

```
/* myfile.h */
# ifndef __myfile_h
    # define __myfile_h
```

```
myfunc( )
{
    /* some code */
}
```
endif

First time the file 'myfile.h' gets included, the preprocessor checks whether a macro called **__myfile_h** has been defined or not. If it has not been, then it gets defined and the rest of the code gets included. Next time we attempt to include the same file, the inclusion is prevented since **__myfile_h** already stands defined. Note that there is nothing special about **__myfile_h**. In its place, we can use any other macro as well.

Command-line Arguments

If we are to write a file-copy program, instead of the program prompting us to enter the source and target filenames, we must be able to supply them at command prompt, in the form:

filecopy PR1.C PR2.C

where, PR1.C is the source filename and PR2.C is the target filename.

This means that we should pass the source filename and target filename to the function **main( )**. This is illustrated in the program given below.

```
# include <stdio.h>
# include <stdlib.h>
int main ( int  argc, char  *argv[ ] )
{
    FILE *fs, *ft ;
    char  ch ;

    if ( argc != 3 )
    {
        puts ( "Improper number of arguments\n" ) ;
        exit ( 1 ) ;
    }

    fs = fopen ( argv[ 1 ], "r" ) ;
    if ( fs == NULL )
```

```
    {
        puts ( "Cannot open source file\n" ) ;
        exit ( 2 ) ;
    }

    ft = fopen ( argv[ 2 ], "w" ) ;
    if ( ft == NULL )
    {
        puts ( "Cannot open target file\n" ) ;
        fclose ( fs ) ;
        exit ( 3 ) ;
    }

    while ( 1 )
    {
        ch = fgetc ( fs ) ;

        if ( ch == EOF )
            break ;
        else
            fputc ( ch, ft ) ;
    }

    fclose ( fs ) ;
    fclose ( ft ) ;
    return 0 ;
}
```

The arguments that we pass on to **main( )** at the command prompt are called command-line arguments. The function **main( )** can have two arguments, traditionally named as **argc** and **argv**. Out of these, **argv** is an array of pointers to strings and **argc** is an **int** whose value is equal to the number of strings to which **argv** points. When the program is executed, the strings on the command line are passed to **main( )**. More precisely, the strings at the command line are stored in memory and address of the first string is stored in **argv[0]**, address of the second string is stored in **argv[1]** and so on. The argument **argc** is set to the number of strings given on the command line. For example, in our sample program, if at the command prompt we give,

filecopy PR1.C PR2.C

then,

argc would contain 3
argv[0] would contain base address of the string "filecopy"
argv[1] would contain base address of the string "PR1.C"
argv[2] would contain base address of the string "PR2.C"

Whenever we pass arguments to **main( )**, it is a good habit to check whether the correct number of arguments have been passed on to **main( )** or not. In our program this has been done through,

```
if ( argc != 3 )
{
    puts ( "Improper number of arguments\n" ) ;
    exit ( 1 ) ;
}
```

Rest of the program is simple. It merely reads every character from source file and writes it into target file.

Exercise

[A] What will be the output of the following programs:

(a)
```c
# include <stdio.h>
void fun ( int *, int * ) ;
int main( )
{
    int  i = 5, j = 2 ;
    fun ( &i, &j ) ;
    printf ( "%d %d\n", i, j ) ;
    return 0 ;
}
void fun ( int  *i, int  *j )
{
    *i = *i * *i ;
    *j = *j * *j ;
}
```

(b)
```c
# include <stdio.h>
int main( )
{
    float  a = 13.5 ;
    float *b, *c ;
    b = &a ;  /* suppose address of a is 1006 */
    c = b ;
    printf ( "%u %u %u\n", &a, b, c ) ;
    printf ( "%f %f %f %f %f\n", a, *(&a), *&a, *b, *c ) ;
    return 0 ;
}
```

(c)
```c
# include <stdio.h>
int main( )
{
    int  i = 2 ;
    # ifdef DEF
        i *= i ;
    # else
        printf ( "%d\n", i ) ;
    # endif
    return 0 ;
}
```

(d)
```c
# include <stdio.h>
# define PRODUCT(x) ( x * x )
int main( )
{
    int  i = 3, j, k, l ;
    j = PRODUCT( i + 1 ) ;
    k = PRODUCT( i++ ) ;
    l = PRODUCT ( ++i ) ;
    printf ( "%d %d %d %d\n", i, j, k, l ) ;
    return 0 ;
}
```

(e)
```c
# include <stdio.h>
# define PI  3.14
# define AREA( x, y, z )  ( PI * x * x + y * z ) ;

int main( )
{
    float a = AREA ( 1, 5, 8 ) ;
    float b = AREA ( AREA ( 1, 5, 8 ), 4, 5 ) ;
    printf ( " a = %f\n", a ) ;
    printf ( " b = %f\n", b ) ;
    return 0 ;
}
```

[B] Point out the errors, if any, in the following programs:

(a)
```c
# include <stdio.h>
void pass ( int, int ) ;
int main( )
{
    int  i = 135, a = 135, k ;
    k = pass ( i, a ) ;
    printf ( "%d\n", k ) ;
    return 0 ;
}
void pass ( int j, int  b )
int  c ;
{
    c = j + b ;
    return ( c ) ;
}
```

(b)
```c
# include <stdio.h>
void jiaayjo ( int , int )
int main( )
{
    int  p = 23, f = 24 ;
    jiaayjo ( &p, &f ) ;
    printf ( "%d %d\n", p, f ) ;
    return 0 ;
}
void jiaayjo ( int  q, int  g )
{
    q = q + q ;
    g = g + g ;
}
```

(c)
```c
# include <stdio.h>
void check ( int ) ;
int main( )
{
    int  k = 35, z ;
    z = check ( k ) ;
    printf ( "%d\n", z ) ;
    return 0 ;
}
void check ( m )
{
    int  m ;
    if ( m > 40 )
        return ( 1 ) ;
    else
        return ( 0 ) ;
}
```

(d)
```c
# include <stdio.h>
void function ( int  * ) ;
int main( )
{
    int  i = 35, *z ;
    z = function ( &i ) ;
    printf ( "%d\n", z ) ;
    return 0 ;
}
```

```
void function ( int *m )
{
   return ( *m + 2 ) ;
}
```

(e)
```
# include <stdio.h>
int main ( int ac, char ( * ) av[ ] )
{
   printf ( "%d\n", ac ) ;
   printf ( "%s\n", av[ 0 ] ) ;
   return 0 ;
}
```

[C] Attempt the following:

(a) Write a function that receives 5 integers and returns the sum, average and standard deviation of these numbers. Call this function from **main( )** and print the results in **main( )**.

(b) Write a function that receives marks received by a student in 3 subjects and returns the average and percentage of these marks. Call this function from **main( )** and print the results in **main( )**.

(c) Write a program using command line arguments to search for a word in a file and replace it with the specified word. The usage of the program is shown below.

C> change <old word> <new word> <filename>

(d) Write a program that can be used at command prompt as a calculating utility. The usage of the program is shown below.

C> calc <switch> <n> <m>

Where, **n** and **m** are two integer operands. **switch** can be any one of the arithmetic or comparison operators. If arithmetic operator is supplied, the output should be the result of the operation. If comparison operator is supplied then the output should be **True** or **False**.

Unit 6

Practice Programs

No matter how much theory you read about programming, there is nothing like actually trying programs yourselves. With that motive I have given below some programming problems and their solutions. Do attempt to write the programs on your own and then check your solution against the solution given here. Happy programming!

Problem 1

If the marks obtained by a student in five different subjects are input through the keyboard, write a program to find out the aggregate marks and percentage marks obtained by the student. Assume that the maximum marks that can be obtained by a student in each subject is 100.

Solution

```c
/* Calculation of aggregate & percentage marks */
# include <stdio.h>
int main( )
{
    int  m1, m2, m3, m4, m5, aggr ;
    float  per ;

    printf ( "\nEnter marks in 5 subjects: " ) ;
    scanf ( "%d %d %d %d %d", &m1, &m2, &m3, &m4, &m5 ) ;

    aggr = m1 + m2 + m3 + m4 + m5 ;
    per = aggr / 5 ;

    printf ( "Aggregate Marks = %d\n", aggr ) ;
    printf ( "Percentage Marks = %f\n", per ) ;

    return 0 ;
}
```

Problem 2

Temperature of a city in Fahrenheit degrees is input through the keyboard. Write a program to convert this temperature into Centigrade degrees.

Solution

```
/* Calculation of simple interest and compound interest */
# include <stdio.h>

int main( )
{
    int  p, n ;
    float  r, si, ci, amt ;

    p = 1000 ;
    n = 3 ;
    r = 8.5 ;

    /*  simple interest */
    si = p * n * r / 100 ;

    /* compound interest */
    amt = p * pow ( ( 1 + r / 100 ), n ) ;
    ci = amt - p ;

    printf ( "Simple interest = Rs. %f\n" , si ) ;
    printf ( "Compound interest = Rs. %f\n" , ci ) ;

    return 0 ;
}
```

Problem 3

The length & breadth of a rectangle and radius of a circle are input through the keyboard. Write a program to calculate the area & perimeter of the rectangle, and the area & circumference of the circle.

Solution

```
/* Calculation of perimeter & area of rectangle and circle */
# include <stdio.h>
int main( )
{
    int  l, b, r, area1, perimeter ;
    float  area2, circum ;
```

```
        printf ( "\nEnter Length & Breadth of Rectangle: " ) ;
        scanf ( "%d %d", &l, &b ) ;
        area1 = l * b ;  /* Area of a rectangle */
        perimeter = 2 * l + 2 * b ;  /* Perimeter of a rectangle */

        printf ( "Area of Rectangle = %d\n", area1 ) ;
        printf ( "Perimeter of Rectangle = %d\n", perimeter) ;

        printf ( "\n\nEnter Radius of circle: " ) ;
        scanf ( "%d", &r ) ;

        area2 = 3.14 * r * r ;  /* Area of Circle */
        circum = 2 * 3.14 * r ;  /* Circumference of a circle */

        printf ( "Area of Circle = %f\n", area2 ) ;
        printf ( "Circumference of Circle = %f\n", circum ) ;

        return 0 ;
    }
```

Problem 4

Temperature of a city in Fahrenheit degrees is input through the keyboard. Write a program to convert this temperature into Centigrade degrees.

Solution

```
/* Conversion of temperature from Fahrenheit to Centigrade */
# include <stdio.h>
int main( )
{
    float  fr, cent ;
    printf ( "\nEnter the temperature (F): " ) ;
    scanf ( "%f", &fr ) ;

    cent = 5.0 / 9.0 * ( fr - 32 ) ;
    printf ( "Temperature in centigrade = %f\n", cent ) ;

    return 0 ;
}
```

Problem 5

Two numbers are input through the keyboard into two locations C and D. Write a program to interchange the contents of C and D.

Solution

```
/* Interchanging of contents of two variables c & d */
# include <stdio.h>
int main( )
{
    int  c, d, e ;

    printf ( "\nEnter the number at location C: " ) ;
    scanf ( "%d", &c ) ;
    printf ( "\nEnter the number at location D: " ) ;
    scanf ( "%d", &d ) ;

    /* Interchange contents of two variables using a third variable as
      temporary store */
    e = c ;
    c = d ;
    d = e ;

    printf ( "New Number at location C = %d\n", c ) ;
    printf ( "New Number at location D = %d\n", d ) ;

    return 0 ;
}
```

Problem 6

Write a program that checks whether two numbers entered by the user are equal or not.

Solution

```
/* Check whether two numbers entered by user are equal or not */
# include <stdio.h>
int main( )
{
```

```
    int  c, d, e ;

    printf ( "\nEnter the number at location C: " ) ;
    scanf ( "%d", &c ) ;
    printf ( "\nEnter the number at location D: " ) ;
    scanf ( "%d", &d ) ;

    if ( c == d )
        printf ( "The two numbers are equal\n") ;
    else
        printf ( "The two numbers are unequal\n") ;

    return 0 ;
}
```

Problem 7

If three numbers are entered through the keyboard, write a program to find out the greatest number.

Solution

```
/* Find greatest of three numbers */
# include <stdio.h>
int main( )
{
    int  a, b, c, big ;

    printf ( "\nEnter three numbers:\n" ) ;
    scanf ( "%d %d %d", &a, &b, &c ) ;

    big = a ;
    if ( b > big )
        big = b ;

    if ( c > big )
        big = c ;

    printf ( "Biggest number = %d\n", big ) ;

    return 0 ;
```

```
    }
```

Problem 8

If a number is entered through the keyboard, write a program to find out whether the number is odd or even.

Solution

```c
/* Find odd or even */
# include <stdio.h>
int main( )
{
    int num ;

    printf ( "\nEnter a number:\n" ) ;
    scanf ( "%d", &num ) ;

    if ( num % 2 == 0 )
        printf ( "Even number\n") ;
    else
        printf ( "Odd number\n") ;

    return 0 ;
}
```

Problem 9

Any year is input through the keyboard. Write a program to determine whether the year is a leap year or not.

Solution

```c
/* Check whether the year is leap or not */
/* Year is Leap if it is a century year and is divisible by 400 */
/* Year is Leap if it is a non-century year and is divisible by 4 */
# include <stdio.h>

int main( )
{
    int yr ;
```

```
    printf ( "\nEnter a year:" ) ;
    scanf ( "%d", &yr ) ;

    if ( yr % 100 == 0 )
    {
        if ( yr % 400 == 0 )
            printf ( "Leap year\n" ) ;
        else
            printf ( "Not a Leap year\n" ) ;
    }
    else
    {
        if ( yr % 4 == 0 )
            printf ( "Leap year\n" ) ;
        else
            printf ( "Not a leap year\n" ) ;
    }

    return 0 ;
}
```

Problem 10

If the marks obtained by a student in five different subjects are input through the keyboard, write a program to print grades according to the following criterion:

Between 90-100% - A Grade

Between 80-90% - B Grade

Between 60-80% - C Grade

Below 60% - D Grade

Solution

```
/* Determination of Grade */
# include <stdio.h>
int main( )
{
    int  m1, m2, m3, m4, m5 ;
    float  per ;
```

```
        printf ( "\nEnter marks in 5 subjects: " ) ;
        scanf ( "%d %d %d %d %d", &m1, &m2, &m3, &m4, &m5 ) ;

        per = ( m1 + m2 + m3 + m4 + m5 ) / 5.0 ;

        if ( per >= 90 && per <= 100 )
            printf ( "A Grade\n" ) ;

        if ( per >= 80 && per < 90 )
            printf ( "B Grade\n" ) ;

        if ( per >= 60 && per < 80 )
            printf ( "C Grade\n" ) ;

        if ( per < 60 )
            printf ( "D Grade\n" ) ;

        return 0 ;
}
```

Problem 11

Write a program that receives two operands and an operator as input and performs the operation and prints the result. Use switch statement.

Solution

```
/* Different operations based on operator */
# include <stdio.h>
int main( )
{
    char operator ;
    int n1, n2, result ;

    printf ( "Enter operator:\n" ) ;
    scanf ( "%c", &operator ) ;

    printf ( "Enter two operands:\n" ) ;
    scanf ( "%d %d", &n1, &n2 ) ;
```

```
switch ( operator )
{
    case '+' :
        result = n1 + n2 ;
        break ;
    case '-' :
        result = n1 - n2 ;
        break ;
    case '*' :
        result = n1 * n2 ;
        break ;
    case '/' :
        result = n1 / n2 ;
        break ;
    case '%' :
        result = n1 % n2 ;
        break ;
    default :
        printf ( "Illegal operator\n" ) ;
}

printf ( "Result = %d\n", result ) ;

return 0 ;
}
```

Problem 12

Write a program to print sum of all numbers up to a given number.

Solution

```
/* Sum up to a given number */
# include <stdio.h>
int main( )
{
    int n, i, sum ;

    printf ( "Enter number:\n" ) ;
    scanf ( "%c", &n ) ;
```

```
    sum = 0 ;
    for ( i = 1 ; i <= n ; i++ )
        sum = sum + i ;

    printf ( "Sum = %d\n", sum ) ;

    return 0 ;
}
```

Problem 13

Write a program to find out the factorial value of a given number.

Solution

```
/* Obtain factorial value of a number */
# include <stdio.h>
int main( )
{
    int  num, fact, i ;

    printf ( "Enter any number:\n" ) ;
    scanf ( "%d", &num ) ;

    fact = 1 ;

    for ( i = 1 ; i <= num ; i++ )
        fact = fact * i ;

    printf ( "Factorial value = %d\n", fact ) ;
    return 0 ;
}
```

Problem 14

Write a program to find out sum of odd and even numbers from 1 to N.

Solution

```
/* Sum of all odds and evens up to N */
# include <stdio.h>
```

```
int main( )
{
    int  num, oddsum, evensum, i ;

    printf ( "Enter any number:\n" ) ;
    scanf ( "%d", &num ) ;

    oddsum = 0 ;
    evensum = 0 ;

    for ( i = 1 ; i <= num ; i++ )
    {
        if ( i % 2 == 0 )
            evensum = evensum + i ;
        else
            oddsum = oddsum + i ;
    }

    printf ( "Sum of odd numbers = %d\n", oddsum ) ;
    printf ( "Sum of even numbers = %d\n", evensum ) ;

    return 0 ;
}
```

Problem 15

Write a program to print the Fibonacci series up to N terms.

Solution

```
/* Print Fibonacci Series up to N terms */
# include <stdio.h>
int main( )
{
    int  num, old, new, term, i ;

    printf ( "Enter any number:\n" ) ;
    scanf ( "%d", &num ) ;

    old = 1 ;
    new = 1 ;
```

```
    printf ( "%d ", old ) ;
    printf ( "%d ", new ) ;

    for ( i = 3 ; i <= num ; i++ )
    {
        term = old + new ;
        printf ( "%d ", term ) ;
        old = new ;
        new = term ;
    }

    return 0 ;
}
```

Problem 16

If a number is input through the keyboard, write a program to find out whether the number is prime or not.

Solution

```
/* Check prime or not */
# include <stdio.h>
int main( )
{
    int  num, i ;

    printf ( "Enter any number:\n" ) ;
    scanf ( "%d", &num ) ;

    if ( n == 1 )
        printf ( "Prime number\n" ) ;
    else
    {
        for ( i = 2 ; i < n ; i++ )
        {
            if ( n % i == 0 )
            {
                printf ( "Not a prime number\n" ) ;
                break ;
```

```
        }
    }

    if ( i == n )
        printf ( "Prime number\n" ) ;
}

return 0 ;
}
```

Problem 17

If a number is input through the keyboard, write a program to calculate the sum of its digits.

Solution

```
/* Sum of digits of a number */
# include <stdio.h>
int main( )
{
    int num, d, sum ;

    printf ( "\nEnter a number(less than 32767): " ) ;
    scanf ( "%d", &num ) ;

    sum = 0 ;
    while ( num != 0 )
    {
        d = num % 10 ;  /* last digit extracted as remainder */
        num = num / 10 ;  /* remaining digits */
        sum = sum + d ;
    }

    printf ( "The sum of digits of %d is %d\n", num, sum ) ;

    return 0 ;
}
```

Problem 18

If a five-digit number is input through the keyboard, write a program to reverse the number.

Solution

```
/* Reverse digits of a 5-digit number */
# include <stdio.h>
int main( )
{
    int  n, a, b ;
    long int  revnum = 0 ;

    printf ( "\nEnter a five digit number (less than 32767): " ) ;
    scanf ( "%d", &n ) ;

    a = n % 10 ;
    n = n / 10 ;
    revnum = revnum + a * 10000L ;

    a = n % 10 ;
    n = n / 10 ;
    revnum = revnum + a * 1000 ;

    a = n % 10 ;
    n = n / 10 ;
    revnum = revnum + a * 100 ;

    a = n % 10 ;
    n = n / 10 ;
    revnum = revnum + a * 10 ;

    a = n % 10 ;  /* 1 st digit */
    revnum = revnum + a ;

    printf ( "The reversed number is %ld\n", revnum ) ;

    return 0 ;
}
```

Problem 19

Write a program to print out all Armstrong numbers between 1 and 100. If sum of cubes of each digit of the number is equal to the number itself, then the number is called an Armstrong number. For example, 153 = (1 * 1 * 1) + (5 * 5 * 5) + (3 * 3 * 3)

Solution

```
/* Generate all Armstrong numbers between 1 & 500 */
# include <stdio.h>
int main( )
{
    int  i = 1, a, b, c ;

    printf ( "Armstrong numbers between 1 & 100 are:\n" ) ;

    while ( i <= 100 )
    {
        a = i % 10 ;  /* extract last digit */
        b = i % 100 ;
        b = ( b - a ) / 10 ;  /* extract second digit */
        c = i / 100 ;  /* extract first digit */

        if ( ( a * a * a ) + ( b * b * b ) + ( c * c * c ) == i )
            printf ( "%d\n", i ) ;

        i++ ;
    }

    return 0 ;
}
```

Problem 20

Write a program to find binary equivalent of a decimal number.

Solution

```
/* Binary equivalent of a decimal number */
# include <stdio.h>
```

```
int binary ( int ) ;
int main( )
{
    int  num ;

    printf ( "\nEnter the number: " ) ;
    scanf ( "%d", &num ) ;

    binary ( num ) ;  /* Function call */

    return 0 ;
}

/* function to convert decimal to binary */
int binary ( int  n )
{
    int  r ;

    r = n % 2 ;
    n = n / 2 ;
    if ( n == 0 )
    {
        printf ( "\nThe binary equivalent is %d", r ) ;
        return ( r ) ;
    }
    else
        binary ( n ) ;     /* Recursive call */
    printf ( "%d", r ) ;
}
```

Problem 21

Write a program that receives numbers into an array and finds sum of
these numbers.

Solution

```
/* Sum of array elements */
# include <stdio.h>

int main( )
```

```
{
    int  arr[ 20 ] ;
    int  sum, i ;

    printf ( "Enter 20 numbers:\n" ) ;
    for ( i = 0 ; i < 20 ; i++ )
        scanf ( "%d", &arr[ i ] ) ;

    sum = 0 ;
    for ( i = 0 ; i < 20 ; i++ )
        sum = sum + arr[ i ] ;

    printf ( "Sum of array elements = %d\n", sum ) ;

    return 0 ;
}
```

Problem 22

Write a program that receives equal number of elements into two arrays and then stores the sum of corresponding elements of these two arrays into a third array and prints the sums.

Solution

```
/* Sum of corresponding elements of two arrays */
# include <stdio.h>

int main( )
{
    int  arr1[ 20 ], arr2[ 20 ], arr3[ 20 ] ;
    int  i ;

    printf ( "Enter 20 numbers of first array:\n" ) ;
    for ( i = 0 ; i < 20 ; i++ )
        scanf ( "%d", &arr1[ i ] ) ;

    printf ( "Enter 20 numbers of second array:\n" ) ;
    for ( i = 0 ; i < 20 ; i++ )
        scanf ( "%d", &arr2[ i ] ) ;
```

```
    for ( i = 0 ; i < 20 ; i++ )
    {
        arr3[ i ] = arr1 [ i ] + arr2[ i ] ;
        printf ( "%d\n", arr3[ i ] ) ;
    }

    return 0 ;
}
```

Problem 23

Write a program to find minimum and maximum element of an array.

Solution

```
/* Minimum and maximum element in an array */
# include <stdio.h>

int main( )
{
    int  arr[ 20 ], min, max, i ;

    printf ( "Enter 20 numbers of first array:\n" ) ;
    .for ( i = 0 ; i < 20 ; i++ )
        scanf ( "%d", &arr[ i ] ) ;

    min = arr[ 0 ] ;
    max = arr[ 0 ] ;

    for ( i = 0 ; i < 20 ; i++ )
    {
        if ( arr[ i ] > max )
            max = arr[ i ] ;

        if ( arr[ i ] < min )
            min = arr[ i ] ;
    }

    printf ( "min = %d max = %d\n", min, max ) ;
```

```
    return 0 ;
}
```

www.ingramcontent.com/pod-product-compliance
Lightning Source LLC
LaVergne TN
LVHW022310060326
832902LV00020B/3383